LISTENING

LISTENING

Hannah Merker

April 1994
for
Fran & Saul
Hannah Merker
& OBEENA

HarperCollins*Publishers*

HarperCollins books may be purchased for educational, business, or sales promotional use. For information please write: Special Markets Department, HarperCollins Publishers, Inc., 10 East 53rd Street, New York, NY 10022.

FIRST EDITION

Designed by Jessica Shatan

Library of Congress Cataloging-in-Publication Data

Merker, Hannah.
    Listening / Hannah Merker.—1st ed.
        p.   cm.
    "Portions . . . published in *No Walls of Stone* (1992, Gallaudet University Press, Washington, D.C.)"—T.p. verso.
    ISBN 0-06-017054-9
    1. Listening. 2. Hearing impaired—Biography. 3. Merker, Hannah.
I. Title.
BF323.L5M37 1994   93-36746
153.6'8—dc20

94 95 96 97 98 ❖/HC 10 9 8 7 6 5 4 3 2 1

for Harvey . . .
and, of course,
for Sheena

". . . In our Jewish tradition, we
listen to objects, to trees, to
clouds, to pebbles. I wanted to
listen to those walls, to ask them
what do they remember . . ."

ELIE WIESEL,
New York Times,
January 23, 1986

1

"At a certain point you say to the woods, to the sea, to the
mountains, the world, Now I am ready. Now I will stop and be
wholly attentive. You empty yourself and wait, listening . . . you
wait, you give your life's length to listening."

ANNIE DILLARD,
Teaching a Stone to Talk, 1982

 The world stands still where we are. And that
small piece of planet is ours alone. However clut-
tered in crowds of colleagues and comrades, families, friends, we each receive the messages of earth and
respond to them, from our separate stance.

Sometimes the messages are unclear. Sometimes we do
not receive them at all and so do not respond.

How can you know that the world around me is quiet—
that I do not hear your step behind me, or hear you call my
name from a distance? The silence around me is invisible.
How can you know that the songs of new birds in spring,
the crunch of old leaves, the soft sigh of the west wind, all

subtle sounds that color the day for you, are not there for me? The whirr of a car, the pounding feet of a runner behind us as we walk, the soft slap of rain on a roof are so elementary a part of your perceptions you cannot imagine that for a person at your side they may not exist. How can you know unless I tell you?

And how can I tell you about something that is not there, if part of my mind is asleep, no longer associates sound with a particular circumstance?

So, then, we must talk to each other, listening in our own ways. Perhaps, while walking with me on the beach, or on some sandy shoreside path, you will ask yourself, what do I hear at this moment . . . ?

Perhaps you will touch my arm, so that I will look at you, and you will say, "The wind is whispering in the willow trees . . . ," or "The gulls, there, are screeching over the fishing nets . . . ," or "Someone nearby is playing a violin . . . "

I still will not hear these things, but now I will know they are there, perhaps remember that once I knew without conscious thought that sound is connected to the swaying willow, the gull. The world becomes larger as the mind reawakens to the soaring symphony of everyday life. We have *both* forgotten these sounds are there.

And so this book is about listening . . . about new ways of listening for the hearing and the hearing impaired.

And it is about a brave experiment that risked a great friendship, an experiment that kindled an augmenting ongoing adventure for me, at this still place in the world where I stand.

This morning, my birthday, walking Sheena in our deserted winter boatyard, slipping between high-cradled craft shrouded in blue plastic or grey-white canvas, I stood at the edge of the north embankment, tiptoeing to the rim where the descent is steep, a near-vertical slope down to the sand and mud, the creek at low tide. He was there. He heard us, silent though I thought we were. Lifting easily, long legs straight out behind him, steel-blue wings curved, unflapping, he circled low, landing on a limb of a leafless tree across the creek, barely visible in the blue-grey mist and mizzle and predawn fog.

It was not quite seven, still winter-dark. Without moving I think about sound, what my great blue heron would have heard, what alerted him to our presence. It is a serious game I play, this search for sound, this glancing around me think-ing about the presence of air waves struck, leaving in the vastness something not there before—the soughing sigh of a light wind, the surging swishing swell of a skein of geese lift-ing out of the reeds in the early light, the slow puttering engines of the commercial fishing craft heading out to their fishing grounds on Long Island Sound.

The struck airwaves I cannot hear; messages of their pres-ence come to me nevertheless. The light wind sends lan-guorous ripples across the creek, feels soft on my cheek, lifts the orange tuft between Sheena's ears; the geese cause a com-motion, hundreds gliding from the reeds, lifting in groups of forty or fifty, each gaggle becoming a skein upon flight, intent on finding, for the day, a broad lawn, a pond, a golf course, returning after sunset to our reeds, our protected narrow nook of a creek. I drink my morning coffee, watching for a ruffling in the reeds other than their leaning with the wind, waiting for Sheena's rush to the window, her skyward glance, which tells me they are honking, conversing (Dosoris Pond today—or the town golf course? . . . I imagine their conversation); and the leaving of the fishermen comes to me by the sudden swaying of my boat beneath my feet, rippling creek water fanning outward, reaching our hull. Quite often I can tell which fisherman is heading for the harbor channel by the way my boat moves. No two captains handle their craft alike. I guess before looking . . . is it *Osprey* or *Navigator*, *Minute Made*, *Deliverance*, *Fisher*, *Daisy II*, *Rebecca*, or *Take Five*?

Stepping back from the edge of the embankment, I look around me. I am standing on gravel, surely grating as I walked, crunching as Sheena prances and sniffs. Our feet, uncushioned by wild grass or sand, present in other parts of the boatyard, told our heron "They are here again, in my special place." His beak opened as he rose over the creek, emitting, I know, his loud rasping heronish squawk.

My game enriches my hours, impassions moments with wonder that might otherwise whisk by uneventful, calm. I welcome such times. It is the absent advent of sound giving dimension to my silent world that I do not want to miss.

And my game has a name.

I call it *LISTENING*.

It was twenty-two years ago, late into my second marriage. My husband, a landscaper, always attended the annual professional convention of his field of endeavor, held every January (when business was slow) at a large Catskills resort hotel. I had steadfastedly refused to accompany him, preferring to watch our four children (he had been a widower and I had adopted his two children) romp in the January snow with our growing population of cats. I was then—as I had always been, still am—an atavistic relic: the last sedentary person alive on exercise-conscious Long Island, or maybe the world. I love winter from behind a sealed window. The only sports I indulge in are sailing and walking my dog—both at leisurely paces. Runners on the roads, sailors racing in rough winds all pass me in a surrealistic blur of insane pursuit. Nothing spurs me to speed.

I avoided the conventions where there was no place to curl up with a book. The rooms were uninviting, the crowds boisterous and oh-so-active. Skating, tobogganing, skiing. . . . That year, my marriage shaky, I agreed to attend, packing one entire suitcase with books, bringing my typewriter. To please my husband, I bought ski clothes—bright yellow ski pants and matching jacket (a color I detest and never wear). I would not embarrass him by spending all my time secluded in our room, uninvolved in the joyous activities of the other wives.

There seemed to be only one way down. The T-bar that

had brought me to the top of this icy hill only brought skiers up. I had wanted to let go only seconds into the ascent. Paralyzed with fear, I was more afraid to let go. At the top, I did not know what to do next. I had never been on skis before. What was I doing on a bitterly cold grey January morning at the top of a hill that someone near me was describing as "a sheet of glass"?

Tenebrous tall spreading pine trees cast long somber shadows down the hill, a hill splashed with the colorful garb of skiers slipping with ease from the summit, some falling midway, laughing. If I could fall . . . slide down sitting . . . if . . .

I do not remember leaving the top. Or falling. I do remember being aware of the quiet, the silence, as if everyone had left the hill and I was there alone. I opened my eyes. I was on my back. I could see that people were talking, a movie with the sound system suddenly silenced. And I could not see correctly either. Everything was blurred.

In our room, with the dreadful ski suit removed, what I already knew was ascertained: no bones were broken. I could not walk because I needed a pair of crutches, my own at home. A congenital back problem made it necessary to always have a pair of crutches, and a couple of canes around for the unexpected fall. With a back brace and crutches I would be able to walk. It would be weeks after the concussion before I would begin to sense how seriously damaged my hearing was. The problems with my eye muscles were eventually resolved by prisms in my lenses, correcting double vision. I have been wearing eyeglasses since I was five. Another alteration to their prescription was not upsetting;

neither was the shock to my delicate back. I had gone through worse times.

A small amount of hearing returned. I accepted its slow progress as the process of healing. That small amount of returned hearing would gradually ebb. Communication through perception of sound, and exchange of thought through heard language, are so taken for granted. Is it possible for a hearing person to comprehend the enormity of its absence in someone else? In herself . . . ? How imagine a silent world?

After the accident I returned to the challenging job I loved—on crutches and with new eyeglasses. I was the director of library services for the visually and physically handicapped in Suffolk County (New York), a subregional division of the Library of Congress's services for handicapped readers. I had established this department of library services. Suffolk County handicapped readers had previously depended on the New York City regional library. Special services to eligible Suffolk County readers had been vastly improved by forming a separate division for a handicapped reading population that was growing rapidly. Already, at that time in the mid-seventies, it exceeded the readership of several states.

Library work—especially the challenges of the Reference Department and the sheer fun and delight of bringing this new service to the county—excited me. I loved the political challenges of fund-raising for the service: although the books and magazines on tape and recordings, the machines on which to play them, the braille materials were all free from the government, each library division was responsible for the funding of space, supplies, and personnel. My four teenage children worked for me, and I had several other employees. I did not notice, for a while, my growing difficulties with telephone communication. It was summer, my fourth year with the program. The services had grown so large the department was about to be transferred to the County Library Building.

It was summer. I loved to sail in the evenings. I would come home, serve supper, running out quickly to my brother's beach where I kept my catamaran, the *Yes Yes*. An hour or two sailing on the bay with Barney, my large brindle boxer, the after-supper summer sky a rainbow of ever-changing colors, was more important to me than food.

One night I came home and found four children crying at the foot of the driveway. My husband had told them he wanted a divorce—unless I stopped sailing, stopped working, and started entertaining the way a businessman's wife should.

At the new location of the library services for the handicapped, a new county library director and I were not getting along. One of my blind readers and her husband had just moved to Barbados. They invited me for an extended vacation. I left for a week, later sending my new boss a ham radio message: I was staying for an undetermined length of time. He fired me immediately.

Freedom is intoxicating. On that quiet friendly island I walked on nearly deserted beaches, sailed small skiffs carefully close to coral reefs. It was time to go on to something else.

Weeks later, at home, I found an ideal apartment in an ancient building, happily leaving the many-acred modern home I had never felt attached to, although *I* had found it one day when we were looking for a larger home. I took my piano, my books, my dog, my old but dependable red Chevy convertible, and very little else. I left more than material possessions behind: standing under an old willow, its wispy long yellowing branches brushing mussel-encrusted rocks (Northport Harbor was less than seven feet from my new back door), I watched my husband's employees carry my few belongings into my apartment—and I knew I was leaving forever the compulsion to live ideals that were not mine.

Not long afterward, with my first set of hearing aids, I rejected several excellent job offers and opened a bookshop half a block from my apartment, on the harbor.

One evening six and a half years ago—May 20, 1986, about 7:30 P.M.—I stepped off the good ship *Bette Anne* for a long walk along the beach with Sheena, my hearing guide dog. Sheena snarled aggressively at a large placid creature more than twice her size. Thus I met Lucky and the person he owned, and thus ended what I had considered my independent life of fourteen years, seven of those years as a live-aboard on the northeast shores of Long Island, a fish-shaped piece of land more than one hundred miles long on New York State's southeastern border. I lived afloat alone—with a dog and a constantly fluctuating population of cats.

What actually ended was not my self-directed life, but living alone.

I loved my way of life. I never expected to find anyone willing to share it—a man with whom I would want to share it. Harvey moved in with Lucky, and Oreo, a middle-aged cat. Nine days later my Emily gave birth to three enormous kittens. (Emily left home not long after . . . Motherhood, I guess, was not for her.) This brought our feline population to eleven.

Harvey went about building closets, and a bed that folds into a swing during the daytime, while I typed articles and stories, marked English composition papers written by students who frequently could not spell the name of the town they lived in and who did not care. The bookshop had closed. I was a free-lance writer, an adjunct professor of English at various Long Island universities, and the executive editor of an academic book review publication.

During that first winter together, as the kittens grew larger, Harvey built *Doorstep*, an eight-foot dinghy, inside the houseboat cockpit. On our long evening walks around the harbor, with Lucky and Sheena, we looked at boats for sale in the local marinas and elsewhere. In April, eleven months after we had met, we bought *Haimish*, the thirty-seven-foot sloop we live on. The houseboat became my office. And we still have *Baby*, the twenty-foot sailboat Harvey has had for more than twenty years.

The following April, on a brilliant seventy-five-degree day, with the willow across the creek trailing new-green in a gusty breeze and the swans guarding a nest in the nearby reedgrass, with over one hundred friends and relatives on the deck of *Haimish*, the roof of *Bette Anne*, and the dock in between, we were married on the bow of our home under a chuppah created from an ivory tablecloth crocheted by my first mother-in-law.

2

"A shadow is floating through the moonlight.
Its wings don't make a sound . . . The ear that listens to the owl
believes in death . . .
The owl goes back and forth inside the night, And the night holds
its breath."

RANDALL JARRELL,
The Bat Poet, 1963, 1964

 A nocturnal barn owl sits high in a hollow tree, listening, a ghost-like golden-buff brown bird with a startling large white heart-shaped face. In the darkness his reversible outer toe flicks to another position. His personal radar system has indicated the location of prey. In a moment he will pounce on a mouse, a shrew, a mole, tightening his versatile toes, then swallowing the small creature whole. Owls have exceptionally sharp night vision; however, the barn owl does not depend or even use this faculty on his nightly hunting forages. *Tyto alba*, the barn owl, depends for survival on sound alone.

To locate his prey, as he does, in utter darkness, he is

equipped with more than just keen hearing. The barn owl is able to detect and utilize subtle differences in sound received by each ear. His familiar face (cosmopolitan creature that he is, he has been spotted on every continent and many islands) divides into two parabolas, flat planes of soft white feathers on either side of an arrant aquiline bill. An extra layer of velvety feathers ensures the complete silence of the barn owl's flight. The parabolas are hidden, as are his ears, his secret sound-receiving, sound-amplifying apparatus, concealed by pliant plumes. In addition, his right ear with its opening is tilted slightly upward, his left ear downward. The receiving of the soft patter of mice, the burrowing of a mole, mere whispers in the night, are heard and defined for vertical or horizontal direction. The message travels swiftly along the owl's inner auditory pathway to his brain. Other aspects of his facial anatomy further refine his directional sensitivity. Abruptly *Tyto* flies to the sensed movement, striking at the invisible sound, pinpointing his prey with deadly accuracy. Sometimes called a flying rat-trap, *Tyto alba* can consume nearly 11,000 rodents in his possible ten-year life span.

Monkeys and cats are known to have excellent hearing, though when tested for horizontal acuity, they scored far below the ability of the barn owl. Perhaps that is why my small cat Sarah takes an aerial stance, crouching high on a piling, pouncing from her perch to the water rats scurrying beneath the dock. I watch her. I am listening. In one swift sleek spring, one smooth silent moment, the rat is dead. I see its mouth open as Sarah grasps it. Is it emitting a last feeble squeak? I cannot be certain. I have heard nothing, not even the soft crunch of Sarah landing on the seaweed, but memory tells me a soft crunch occurred. I have watched her and I know the rat is dead. Sarah, though, has not finished giving me her gift. She carries the rat in her teeth, its long tail brushing along the wooden planks of the dock, dropping it on the floor in front of my typewriter.

Humans, according to studies, when consciously listening, can locate sound as skillfully as the barn owl on the azimuth (the horizontal plane). Our accuracy falls dismally short in exactness in detecting sound on the elevation dimension. For a high sense of auditory awareness human beings must mingle visual and intuitive mental cues with the receiving of sound. Unlike the barn owl, our survival does not depend on sound alone. We have untapped depths of flexibility and retraining. It is possible for hearing impaired and deaf people to "hear," to acknowledge cues that indicate the presence of sound. It is possible for us to listen.

Listening is as primeval as man. In the primordial forests of the first living creatures there was no speech, no spoken symbols systematically arranged into significant expression. But there was communication. Before linguistics, before the literal link of language, there was listening.

Dictionaries define the word "listening" as the act of giving attention with the ear; attentive hearing; to give ear to; to try to catch the sound of something. It seems with language we have narrowed the dimensions of the meaning of a word with subtle ramifications affecting everyone's life, every day, every moment. We have defined "listen" strictly within auditory terms.

Without articulate speech original man and other early forms of life communicated by movements, signs and symbols that formed a vocabulary of their own, a method still used by animal life. How was my mother swan able to tell her mate to sit for three days on her last unhatched egg? How did she say to him, "I have sat here for weeks. Now you must stay here while I teach our infants to swim." Communication was—still is—by awareness, by watching, by waiting.

Are such nonverbal messages really primitive? Listening is now being taught as a communication art, as an active rather than a passive experience. It is being taught as a skill that can be learned in schools, in social service therapy, in the private sector of business seminars. Perhaps we are so removed from our beginnings in our mechanized computerized world that we can no longer recognize, or give, a response that was once artless and elemental.

In an essay entitled "How to Attend a Conference," the noted linguist S. I. Hayakawa wrote, ". . . listening requires entering actively and imaginatively into the other person's situation and trying to understand a frame of reference different than your own . . . "

Life has become complicated. We can no longer simply absorb and respond. Will conversation become exhausting beyond the ability to continue using it? Perhaps soon we will long for those bygone days of inarticulate grunts and insensible sounds, mixed with bodily gestures symbolic of thought.

Or perhaps we will see that listening is not a course you must register for, a new gimmick that will magically transform your social and professional life. It happens when you take time to look around you, to be still in the evenings, startled by mornings. To listen means to be aware, to watch, to wait patiently for the next communication clue. And, as anyone with a speech or hearing disability can tell you, listening is not always auditory communication.

How then do we redefine the word "listening" to include all the interacting phenomena that occur when a deaf or hearing impaired person is talking to a friend, walking alone on a beach, occupying her spot in the world on any particular day? The ears of such a one miss much. The wonder that is the human body seems willing to soar over the gap. When earth's auditory energy is received as a whisper, or perhaps not at all, other senses become sharpened, grasping communicative clues we have forgotten, in the rush of life, are there. Listening becomes visual, tactile, intuitive.

Listening . . . perhaps . . . is just a mind aware. . . .

3

"The strands are all there:
to the memory nothing is ever really lost."

EUDORA WELTY,
· One Writer's Beginnings, 1983, 1984

 When we think about hearing, about listening, we instinctively think about the ear. When I am consciously trying to collect and conceive the meaning of a particular sound, my mental response, my collective memory of how sound is known, reaches toward the perceived sensation. Almost imperceptibly my body leans toward what I am trying to capture, giving those flaps of skin on the sides of my head, my outer ears, their best opportunities to perform their singular function—to gather the vibrations falling on the air around me. Still, collecting those vibrations does not ensure mental knowledge of what is happening.

In the ordinary path of things, when all parts of the ear are in perfect accord, an outer ear collects the loudnesses and softnesses of life, and many of the subtleties—the sighs of the wind, the chirping of crickets, the humming of insects, intrusions like the high screech of an ambulance, the buzz of a power saw. And caught, too, are all the myriad musical tones of human conversation, striking the air, setting molecules in motion.

The moving molecules become waves of sound that are funneled by the outer ear to the tympanic membrane (the eardrum), causing it to vibrate.

On the other side of the tympanic membrane is a narrow air-filled chamber, the middle ear. Three tiny bones with fanciful names pick up and enhance the movements of the eardrum, conducting them across the middle ear cavity. The vibrations of these bones—the malleus (hammer), the incus (anvil), and the stapes (stirrup)—arrive in the cochlea, a fluid-filled snail-shaped chamber in the inner ear. Now sound recognition is possible. The inner ear, the true nerve center for hearing, is where sound is prepared for transmission to the brain.

In the labyrinth of the inner ear sound waves that have entered the cochlea are picked up by microscopic sensory receptors, 30,000 hair cells arranged in four rows. They bend, swaying as vibrations are received, relaying impulses to nerve fibers that form the acoustic nerve. It is only when the acoustic nerve transmits the message to the brain that the *concept* of heard sound becomes extant. Now the brain says, Aha! I am knowing the sigh of the wind ... I am knowing the chirping of crickets ... I am knowing the whispered words of a dear human voice. All this transpires in seconds.

The structure of the ear, a long-ago-evolved wonder devised before modern technical expertise, relies on comparatively crude surgical methods to repair its delicate configurations.

In the process of losing hearing one is neither a hearing nor a deaf person. For the hearing impaired person there is a middle place of fog. Sounds reach us that we cannot define. We may be aware that a person is speaking, that a voice or voices are present close by, but be unable to decipher more than an occasional word. We may not be able to be sure from which direction the sound we "sense" is coming. Something inside our head is just not working ... and it is not our thinking processes. They may be functioning in their fine-tuned way with the information received. The problem is that not all information collected by our outer ears is being received inside. At some point the message ceases to be transmitted to the ultimate receiver and interpreter, the brain.

When we think about our ears we usually have in mind those external cartilaginous flaps, sometimes clinging close against the head, sometimes large and leaning outwards. These exterior parts of our anatomy are actually almost entirely useless, appendages that are part of us in the continuum of genetic and evolutionary ancestry.

For once upon a time, long ago, before we learned to live on dry land, we were fish, creatures of the swamps and the seas. Our gills, at that time, took in sounds transmitted through our water world. That was perhaps 260 million years ago . . . just history in our mind-world . . . but still fact in our physical world.

When our first ancestors began to adapt to life on land, when they began to grasp oxygen from the air, their gills changed form, becoming our outer and middle ears. Gills are not capable of perceiving sound. Fish perceive sound waves through their acute sense of balance. Any fisherman will tell you that noises above water will not disturb the silent swimmers beneath the surface. Water changes—a splash or surging swell creating underwater sound waves—inform a fish to be aware. The water movement is felt in the part of the gills that controls equilibrium.

How remarkable that a water-world still controls our ability to hear, for sound airborne from anywhere must enter and be acknowledged by our fluid-filled inner ear before being transferred to nerve impulses that will recognize the disturbance as "sound." And so, loss of the outer ear affects only the visual perspective of what we expect a human being to look like. It does not affect hearing.

When does hearing begin? When does the perception of auditory phenomena happen, with all its range of calm or clamor, humming or hubbub, timbre and tone? When does a human being begin to listen?

By the twenty-eighth day after conception the ear capsule is forming in the human embryo. Its dimensions, the space for it, will be of adult size before birth. Rudimentary gills appear in the beginning child at the sides of the head, reminders that our ultimate beginnings, our most ancient ancestors, were water creatures.

In the seventh week of growing the middle chambers of the embryonic human's ears become functionally alive. The most significant aspect of this development is that a sense of stability has become part of the becoming human being. The embryo can now balance itself within the womb. The inner ear communicates with structures that provide static equilibrium throughout life. This happening in the seventh to eighth week after fertilization of the egg is a fortuitous gift of heritage. In our early aquatic life forms, as in fishes now, equilibrium is more important than hearing. The perception of sound evolved at a later evolutionary state, as it will in the prenatal child.

In the twelfth week of embryonic life, hearing-nerve endings develop in the inner ear. The primitive gills will soon become the outer and middle ears, the receivers and transmitters of sound to the delicate sensitive mechanism in the labyrinths and canals of the inner ear. The snail-shaped cochlea with its minute turns, twists, and follicles becomes fully formed in the fifth month of human gestation. Yet . . . hearing does not happen.

The sensing and interpreting of sound in the embryonic child happens after the growing fetus relives the miracles of change over millions of years of life forms. In nine months the embryonic child's form flies through time, through uncountable space, magically modifying to modern needs, all while living in a liquid world as did its prehistoric ancestors. The beginning child briefly relives all our tentative life forms, starting with the single-cell life form of many millions of years past.

In the seventh month of pre-outer-world life the entire human auditory apparatus will be ready to conduct, receive, acknowledge sound.

Growing evidence confirms that in the normal prenatal human being auditory receptors can be stimulated. Sound stimuli can pass through the mother and through the membrane and liquids surrounding the fetus.

Recent experiments report that, at the start of the third trimester of pregnancy, blinking occurs in response to sound stimuli. The floating child can even exhibit selective attention, tuning out stimuli it finds annoyingly repetitive or disturbing. Three months before it leaves its water world, a human being is listening.

Does the incipient person know to what it is listening during the moments it is aware of sound? Probably not ... but the highly developed nervous system of the seven-month-old human fetus can be affected by what is pleasant or disagreeable. It can discriminate between, and sometimes remember, what is acceptable in its resting environment, and noise that is objectionable. The ear's sensitivity to tiny differences in the pitch or intensity of sound gives it fine discriminatory powers. Loudness, timbre, resonance, vibrations, a trumpet blast, a barely audible murmur are taken in by the ear and translated into meanings and happenings of immediate surrounding life.

A recent experiment was conducted wherein pregnant mothers read aloud fairy tales and children's stories to their unborn children. After birth, the same tales were read to the infants by their mothers and fathers. The children invariably responded to their mothers' readings, and seemingly were unresponsive to the voices of their fathers or anyone else.

Did each recognize a mother's voice? Were they listening in that other world? Or did sound waves from the mother's voice traveling down her spine somehow reverberate and later create recognition? The only conclusions at present are that some connection, some vital recognition, took place. It was not a rejection of the father but rather a response to something familiar.

Dr. Harvey J. Gardner, director of the Huntington (New York) Hearing and Speech Center, describes the essence of listening as ". . . a state when one does not know one is listening . . . one is spontaneous, no longer conscious of self . . . it is a form of ego loss when there is no barrier between you and someone else."

Perhaps in our prebirth state we are ultimate listeners, with no ego to lose, allowing messages to travel on sound waves to our receptors in the inner ear, unimpeded, at first, by prejudices that will inevitably develop in our adult minds.

Are we only really listening when we allow ourselves to accept, without judgment, what another is saying? And . . . is this possible? We know the seven-month-old-almost-child rejects sound that is unpleasant. A recognition has taken place between pleasure and pain—between noise and other kinds of sound. In our earliest environment, sheltered as it is, a snug safe sea, we express signs of self, inclinations of individual thinking.

We are born judgmental, expressing ourselves vociferously at our first moment in limitless space with a cry in a nonverbal language. Is it a sound expressing sadness or joy, sorrow or satisfaction, anguish or enchantment? Or is it nothing else, as it is said, but the new infant exercising his lungs in the medium he has, until that moment, not known—air?

How can we know? No one, as yet, has written about their first utterance. No one has told us the meaning of that first vocalization, the birth cry.

4

"It is all too easy to take language, one's own language, for granted—one may need to encounter another language, or rather another mode of language, in order to be astonished, pushed into wonder, again."

OLIVER SACKS,
Seeing Voices: A Journey into the World of the Deaf, 1989

 First we need language, images intimating the intelligence, the information impressed on our conscious selves. We need something that translates messages to understanding, in a conceptual medium that illuminates and deciphers the communications we are receiving. We need what is variously defined as that "aspect of human behavior that involves the use of vocal sounds in meaningful patterns and, when they exist, corresponding written symbols to form, express, and communicate thoughts and feelings"; "... any method of communicating ideas, as by a system of signs, symbols, gestures, or the like ..."; "... the transmission of meaning, feeling, or intent ... the manner or means of communications between living creatures ..."

We need language.

Language encompasses far more than just words. It begins with labels, sounds, names of things, individual identification of people, objects, ideas, happenings, stark unadorned letter-combinations that click in our mind when read or heard with something learned at some point in our lives. We see or hear *chair, bed, house, man, woman, baby,* and we immediately know what that letter combination means, even when the ramifications of the word, the possible conceptions of it, are infinite. How varied chair, bed, house, man, woman, baby can be in aesthetic imagination and random design, yet we know what another person means when these words are transferred to us. We have understanding.

After labels, which are sometimes generalities, we want to convey specifics, give dimension and specialness to the chair, the house, the baby. The descriptive language of words and gestures gives us color and depth, affinities and antipathies, allusions to read or receive, impressions that, in an instant, resonate in the room of memory and return to the moment, enlarged by preknowledge. We have understanding.

So then, when we listen ... when we are really listening ... we are not just hearing. Hearing, after all, is merely receiving, the brain's recognition of sound, something that will happen without personal will, unless our hearing mechanism is defective or temporarily denied access by earplugs, by sorrow, by some acute concentration that shuts off our sensibilities. Listening happens when we are attentive, when we choose responsibly to receive *and* understand an earth message of some kind. Listening is a conscious act.

It seems so simple . . . we have language with nuances that create fatter and fatter dictionaries . . .

We have perception that allows us to touch the moon . . .

Yet often we cannot touch each other or the world around us . . .

We have forgotten how to listen . . .

Mathematics ripples through our language life, raising realities to visual or imagined form, connecting concepts and ideas with unimagined measurements. To realities we give linear line the latitude to go up and down, across and in. We have height and width and depth, a three-dimensional expanse of size set in a comparative setting, thus known by its relative largeness or smallness, its capacity in terms of bulk. Sometimes there is a fourth dimension, time, thus placing the measured thing in yesterday, or tomorrow.

Ideas and concepts also have proportions, their content and caliber, their stretch and sweep and scope quite measurable in another spatial sphere. Height and width and depth take on new meaning in the realm of thought, imagery, perception. Their visual manifestation, language, is the tool used to give dimension and individuality to thinking, a reality that does not fill physical space.

So we are back to mathematics. How do we quantify something that is not touchable, something that lacks the knowing learned by tactile or visual impact? How do we begin to evaluate abstractions such as hearing, listening, understanding, attention? How do we assign numbers of degree, percentages of internal intake to concepts that have word labels, each with a variety of meanings? We need definitions, amplifications, which divide the significant possibilities of the whole of an idea into its random aspects.

We could begin with music, a measured presence, monitored in the fourth dimension, by time. Music right away is otherworldly. It is the language of music that gives sound its form-reality, that separates what could be (and sometimes is) just noise riding air waves from intellectual recognition. Mathematics shapes music, creating its language since the mid-seventeenth century.

We call a group of notes within a time frame, from one strong accent to the next, a measure. It is a standard of time calculation between two bars on a written musical page. Perhaps the measure has been written to be played in one second, or perhaps two seconds, or half a second. The notations on a sheet of music indicating timing tell us what vision the composer heard within the creative recesses where new thinking occurs.

In a measure of music, or poetry, we can hear a brief theme, a movement characterized by a rhythm. Thus a deaf musician can read a musical score, "hearing" with the inner ear of previous knowledge sounds that cannot reach him. Gabriel Urbain Fauré continued composing his church and chamber music long after he could no longer identify their sound. And dear Ludwig (van Beethoven), who dreamed of being called a "tone poet," rose to creative heights of melody and composition in his last five quartets undiminished by his inability to audibly perceive his own music. Imagination transcended deafness, rendering him capable of "listening" to the notes he put on paper, a cerebral exercise but nevertheless a real one. For music is sound transformed into art, set in a structure of time and intensity, depth and color, with random variations within a time frame expressing the emotions, the ideas of the artist.

In memory I can hear the soft gentle notes of a Chopin nocturne, the opening thoughts of any Beethoven sonata, the counterpoint of a Bach fugue with its complicated interwoven voices. Each form has a mathematical precision within which a musician created anew the sensing possibilities of a certain number of sounds. It is a language like any other. (With only twenty-six letters we have invented, in English, over a million words.)

In actuality, now, I hear very few of the notes of a nocturne, a sonata, a fugue, but I can see the melodies in the air, setting the invisible ether into motion. Vibrations are caught by my outer ear, undulating to my eardrum and then . . . there is a disconnection. Still, the distant musician, perhaps deaf Fauré or Beethoven, speaks across time to a hearing impaired "listener." Reading a score or remembering I am knowing the sadnesses, the joys, the impressions a piece evokes. I am connected to some musician and his creations by language.

I am listening.

"We listen to Bach transfixed because this is listening to a human mind."

LEWIS THOMAS, The Medusa and the Snail, 1979

Beyond the barriers of bad connections that have lessened loudnesses, softened all once-known sound, beyond the sameness of too many silences, I look for language.

I find it everywhere.

All languages have one intent: communication. A language is a capturing in symbols of idioms of individual behavior, thinking, feeling, yearning. There are written and unwritten languages, some with many word symbols, others with few, amplifed by gestures, yet so explicit in expression that they accomplish the same goal as those with thousands of verbal nuances.

The mathematics of musical notation transfers the sound of music into a written language. Can that written language transmit the *emotion* of sound? The singular intent of the composer? The varied imaginings of thematic rendition that flow from the musician's instrument? Can symbols on paper become alive, stirring the air, moving air molecules in patterns that quicken our senses, kindle the kinetic energy of emotional and intellectual response, if we cannot hear them? Perhaps.

The auditory impact of music on the brain challenges the interest of scientists in a new way. Music has long been considered a language of the emotions, an artistic translation of a physical phenomenon—feelings. Researchers are intrigued by the brain's reaction to common pitch intervals, to tempo, to rhythm. Listeners have been tested for changes in heart rate and other physical indicators of emotional response. Current research has compared differing levels of human response to a radio with separate controls for volume and tone; emotional reactions are on two separate independent levels—pleasantness and intensity.

A report on this research invites us to imagine that listeners have internal maps, byways to the known. Beethoven could scrawl across a blank page the enormity of the opening tones of his Ninth Symphony. A person with limited hearing could read that page, perhaps remembering what once was known sound . . . the moving soaring moments of those first few notes.

Would it be the same as the primary sensation? Can memory move us equal to such auditory moments?

Such comparative listening systems have not yet been tested. The hearing impaired listener, depending on the degree and range of hearing loss, is often aware of great gaps when listening to music. Sometimes I listen to recordings of Chopin's nocturnes, intent on filling in the sudden silences by imagining the score, placing my fingers on an imaginary keyboard, letting my fingers trace the melodies I once played, lyrical phrases I once knew, once could hear. It is an interesting mental exercise, one that used to fill me with a sadness much larger than the richness of the recollected music.

One night a friend had a wonderful inspiration. She brought music back to me through the magic of language, reminding me that there are many ways to listen. She attended an open-air evening concert in a planetarium garden, pencil and paper in hand:

Bach concert
I hear for you.
Sound of a concert piano.
The felt hammer hits the string and the sound comes forth.
The sound is resonated in the perfect warp of wood to give
forth the beautiful continual sound . . . the lovely feeling
and beauty of music on a quiet clear summer night.

The violins and bass strings in the background of the piano
. . . There is a long pause of silence during the music. The
silence is as important as sound, slowly soft low strings of
warm violins pick up the music once again.
Deep somber tones are felt deep in the ear and body.
A light piano key, note by note intermingles the tune and
plays whimsy with the notes.
The piano notes are clear, precise. The strings softly play in
the background.
The piano notes ascend, cascade and then stop as the soft-
muted violins play a section, then mingle with the piano.
Notes slip up and down the keyboard. Sliding fingers give
gaiety to the moment.
The music crescends and builds to full tones and the music
reverses the opening, descending in cascades of notes.
And ends with clear staccato piano notes.
A small plane flies overhead.
The pilot has no idea what beauty of sound he slightly dis-
turbed, what wonderful music he has missed.*

* Joan Coller, ©1985

On another evening Joan recorded for me a concert of a different kind:

> The pleasant relaxing sounds on a warm August evening
> are the crickets and cicadas playing concerts in harmony on
> their legs.
> The cricket chirp is a high pitch, the cicada low as if there
> is not enough resin on the bow string.
> No matter what note or tempo they singularly choose, it
> becomes the harmonious song of the summer night.*

The composer Gustav Mahler once said, "The most important thing in music is not the score." The language of music is so subjective its intent can be conveyed in many ways.

The words used by Joan to describe the two concerts evoked more of an emotional surge of feeling of the happenings than reading a score. Of course, an unscientific element runs through this. I have never read the score of a cicada or cricket concert.

---

* Joan Coller, ©1985

5

"He shrugs. 'I'm listening.' . . . she says . . . 'You listen but
don't hear!' distinguishing, the way the Chinese will, between
effort and result . . . One listens . . . why should a listening
person not hear? What's taken for granted in English . . . is
spelled out in Chinese . . . Ting de jian in Mandarin means
'One listens and hears.' Ting bu jian means 'One listens but
fails to hear' . . . It's an old culture talking.
Everywhere there are limits . . . "

GISH JEN,
Typical American, 1991

 Sometimes the road to Deaf is random, roving
slowly toward that mystical place that is not myth
at all. The weather there is foggy, softening the
shock that we have arrived. Oh, yes, this place is real, and at
first, to new residents, an apparent isolated island. There are
no road signs, no arrows for the occasional visitor, no maps.
In fact, it is so hard to find Deaf Island and the people who
live there. We are invisible—as is our world.

I noticed the world was getting quieter . . . a silence, a
soundlessness was softening the edges of my sometimes strident life. The noticing did not appear in a single startling
revelation. No, it was with a slow astonishing surprise that I

sensed the increasing hush around me, with no glimmer yet of the stunning reality: only *my* world was growing quieter. I was becoming deaf.

When we are used to things, familiar with their presence, we often cease to see them. Or hear them. And silence was something I was becoming used to, an atmosphere once sought in retreat from a large noisy family. Now silence came unbidden, softly, unnoticed, creeping close and staying with me. I noticed the absence of things. My mini-house seemed hushed with the stillness present in a storm when power is cut off. We never hear the heating unit simmering slowly, the whirrings of refrigerators. Machinery around us never really registers in our minds as heard. All the lulling murmurs so part of our indoor space are most noticed when they cease. We never hearken to their sound. Then a sultry summer storm or a blustery wintry blizzard cuts off our power source and we are enclosed in a solemn stillness. No noise was ever so loud.

And so it was, more than twenty years ago, as I huddled in my frigid rented-cottage-with-the-wonderful-view, when it seemed to me the surging sound of winter winds was lessening. From my hilltop windows I could see the squally gusts of a northeaster whipping waves to foam, bending branches low, stirring up and scattering dead autumn leaves. A thought crossed my mind: if I had not got up to close the window, I would not have known a storm was raging outside.

(. . . months later, on an icy windswept January afternoon, I walked a half-frozen beach, possessed by wonder [a wonder that would not last terribly long, yet still catches me breathless when I think of it.] Wearing my newly acquired hearing aids I was amazed by the sound of the incoming tide, astonished by screeching gulls, crunching snow, clinking halyards on winter-beached craft. I had forgotten the presence of all this—the absence engulfing me gradually . . . I had noticed, with more and more acute distress, agitation [fear?], the distance of voices, the vagueness of sounds I could not transfer to intelligent meaning . . . Those sounds are etched in memory, music I would soon know only by alertness to visual cues that announced their presence, songs of the seaside world which were not changing at all. Only *my* ears were changing, barely responding, after a while, to the magic of newer, more powerful hearing aids . . .)

Greyness, the toning down of sound-color to dimness, dullness, the diminishing of resonance, arrives sometimes so slowly, so gently, so subtle is the happening. In the greyness there began to be a tumult of a special kind . . . annoyance, anger (. . . "Why don't you answer your telephone?" or " . . . You're not listening to me . . . " And one day at an intersection, stopped at a red light: "Hey, lady, doncha know there's an ambulance behind ya? Ya deaf or somethin'? . . . ") The world was no longer limitless. I felt the pressure of unseen walls. I left the telephone unplugged in the evenings.

In the safeness of my tiny cottage, in the ascending silence, surrounded by my many cats and Barney, my old dog, I retreated from a vague disturbing discomfort. Here no one questioned my attention. It was to be a while yet before I realized that for some time Barney had been telling me when someone was at the door.

Luckily one day I succumbed to the flu. I sat slumped in a chair, my physician staring at an artistic grey-white study of my chest cavity on the opposite wall. Soon he was facing me, shaking my shoulders, saying, "You didn't hear a word I said." I did not realize, at first, that he just mouthed the words, no sound uttered. Automatically I read his lips, as I must have been unconsciously doing for some time. He was testing me, and of course he was correct. I had not heard a word he had said.

When was it, when did I first realize that my large brindle boxer was telling me when there was a knock at our door, when the telephone rang, when an erratic sound was present around me? As we walked at dawn, at dusk, I was pushed to one side if a car surged behind us; I was awakened as the sun rose by a lick on my face. When did the radio and the alarm clock cease to register to my senses as heard?

My dog was old, quite ill, yet I clung to this creature that most understood my muffled world. What would I do without him? Attached to me as he was since a pup, Barney had become my ears, interpreting sounds around me, conveying to me life messages one sense did not receive.

It is not unusual for animals to attach themselves to a person, responding to that person's specific needs. An amazing connection can take place over the years. I was besieged by nightmare thoughts of training a new dog, something I thought beyond what I could do, something I needed now. I had heard of a place in Colorado that trained dogs for the hearing impaired, to perceive the needs of people whose world had become increasingly silent. Perhaps, I thought, I should contact them . . .

I was living on the good ship *Bette Anne* now, the twenty-one windows of the mini-cottage-with-the-wonderful-view a mere glimpse through summer-leafed trees. Had a guide dog ever been trained to live asea? I contacted the Guide Dog Foundation for the Blind, a nearby training center. Magic happens. They had recently been given an anonymous grant to train several dogs for the hearing impaired. Their trainers came to see me, watching my ways of handling my seriously ill dog and my several cats. They needed to know me and my environment in order to choose the most suitable dog for me. They could see that my Barney had become a life-support system for me.

Sheena had already completed training in basic obedience skills. She was skilled, too, in responding to specific sounds, and how to report them. The ring of a telephone, a tap on a door, an alarm clock, a baby crying, would bring her to her owner indicating she had a message to convey. Soon I would see her transfer her allegiance from her trainer to me. But at the beginning, while Barney still lived, only the trainers came to my home. I knew nothing about my future companion. I did not ask.

Unknown to me, Sheena, the dog that had been chosen to be my new ears, was brought to the swaying docks and waterfront life of Port Jefferson, a harbor community not far from my own. She was being prepared to adapt to my specific needs and the unusual things she would need to know living on a boat.

In June I flew to California, to the wedding of my eldest daughter. I did not hear announcements of departures and arrivals. My youngest daughter and I made changes in our homebound flights from San Francisco. My little one, boarding her flight to her college in Seattle, said, "Mama . . . what will you do when I get on my plane?" That year the acuteness of my problem was clear to her. Without her, an hour later, I missed my flight, after a twenty-four hour standby wait. The reservations clerk was alerted to my need for personal contact . . . but it was the night before a possible air controllers' strike. The airport was a mob scene of people trying to get home earlier than planned. I was waiting near the desk. They forgot, just called my name over the loudspeaker. I never heard it.

Barney died at the end of that month, June 1982. A week before, he lost his own hearing. For that week and the days after, until Sheena came to me, I had time to absorb the shocking impact of isolation when certain kinds of communication are cut off. I did not know when a visitor was at my door; I did not hear a leak, one evening, which flooded a room not ten feet away from me.

I remembered the day he had become part of the family fourteen years earlier. I had said, No more dogs. Nevertheless when my husband, children, three friends, and one cat were in our car, about to leave "just to look" at a new litter of boxers, I squeezed into the rear seat.

Ten exuberant pups romped in a woodsy wooden-fenced backyard. I saw one stop and stare at me. Like a newborn infant, his massive head did not yet fit the rest of him. Clear eyes assessed me. His owners deftly dropped him into my arms. "We're just looking," I said. "Of course . . . ," was the understanding reply.

He settled his nose into my armpit as we drove home.

He declared me his person from the very beginning, greeting my appearance each morning and evening as a special wonder in his life, rarely leaving my side when I was at home. The ebbing of sound in my life was eased by my alert loving companion. Somehow he knew I was unaware of much of the audible world around me.

Two years before his death I marveled that Barney was still with us. He and I and the cats were alone now. His steps were slower, his large fine frame more defined as he gradually lost weight. Until his last morning my staunch survivor still leapt aggressively at other dogs, runners, speeding cars, undefined shadows. One day I recognized there was no way to diminish the effects of tumors, heart ailments, failing eyesight, arthritis, old age, and the sad direction of human anger (one night in his last months someone quite drunk threw acid on his back . . .).

I said to him, "Barns, old friend, you are waiting for Laura to come home . . ." He knew, of course, my eldest daughter was on her way from California. We had looked forward to her visit. I knew he would not leave me until she was with me.

On his last morning, he could no longer walk. We carried him to a cushioned car. He held his head high, the only part of him not touched by cancer and the effects of the acid burns. As we carried him into the veterinarian, he snarled at a Saint Bernard.

I coiled his leash in long low loops, setting it softly down beside my fierce fine friend, my longtime comrade, confidant, companion, my protector and interpreter of my muted world. A few moments before I had held that proud head tight against me, my daughter and son-in-law hugging me close, as our veterinarian quickly and mercifully put Barney, my old boxer, into his long permanent sleep.

How could I accept another dog so quickly, a strange creature in our midst? I realized how much time had been spent those last months caring for Barney's wounded wasted shape. He never complained. Until nearly the end he continued to explain the world to me. I called the Guide Dog Foundation. I was ready to meet my new friend.

Sheena, a year-and-a-half-old orange fluff of energy with doe-like eyes, arrived with her trainers, gentle intuitive people. Nothing seemed beyond the scope of their efforts or imagination in the process of Sheena's transition from her kennel life at the Foundation to our particular circumstance. Curious and alert, she impishly tested my orders, which might be a quiet voice command, a hand signal, a certain kind of tug on the leash.

We worked together, learning to live together, with the trainers visiting and helping us often. The edge of efficiency was on her side. She knew what to do. Her training was exceptional. Still, life on the water was a huge Pandora's chest.

Twelve years have gone by. Life is still filled with new wonders for Sheena. She flicks an ear at swooping gulls, flaps a not-too-patient tail at one of our regular evening visitors, a night heron who perches on our stern catwalk at low tide, awaiting the darkest hours to feed in the shallows. She awakens me at odd hours, saying, in our special language, "It is raining, close the port windows . . . " Or she leaps on my bed, paws my shoulders, turning her head back and forth, her eyes from me to the floor. Yes, Sarah, our ten-year-old feline, has brought in another dead water rat. I know there was sound connected to the rat's arrival. Sarah is very clumsy. Leaping through a window, her usual custom after a night's foraging, she knocked over a plant and several books. Sheena, a workaholic, is alert to the world's sounds twenty-four hours a day.

And Sheena goes everywhere with me, enjoying the same rights and privileges as a guide dog for the blind. I now have almost no hearing at all. My dog knows that. She asserts her unique personality, expressive and aware, reporting to me things I should know, simply signaling with a raised ear, a body movement, when something is happening that is normal, such as footsteps on our dock that are known to us, or thunder that is tumbling our windswept waters, or when something is amiss. I cannot hear thunder anymore, had forgotten it was there. Sheena has a special signal for thunder, not a response she was taught. By watching me she has come to know, as Barney did, when I am unaware of something happening.

I cannot hear the rain on our roof, the sound of a car horn, someone walking behind me. Hearing guide dogs are trained to respond to their owner's need by physical contact. A knock on our door brings Sheena racing aflutter to the door, eyes shifting from my face to the door, racing back and forth casting cats and books and who knows what else asunder. If I fail to take note of her important message she will take my hand or skirt and pull gently. We were separated in our first year together for three weeks when Sheena was in the hospital. A car was speeding down the harbor road. I did not notice Sheena's signals, my mind elsewhere. I did not hear warning shouts from nearby people in the boatyard. Sheena threw herself between me and the oncoming car.

Guide dogs for the deaf confer a special love to their persons with each significant cue, infusing us with a sense of security and peace. And we, their persons, are constantly in awe, knowing our hearing dog, this alive aware presence, would not be alive at all, if not for the hearing dog programs that train them. Dogs for the hearing impaired are usually strays or abandoned animals, random-bred mixed breeds found in kennels and dog shelters. (When asked what breed she is, I say she is 100 percent everything.) Though healthy and intelligent they are marked for destruction because there is no room in overcrowded facilities to maintain them. My Sheena, when found and selected by the Guide Dog Foundation, was scheduled for death the next morning.

Most everyday sounds of life simply do not exist for me, and for many like me. Music, conversation, signals of danger, all are vague if noticed at all. Since the training of dogs for the hearing impaired and deaf began in 1976, under the auspices of the American Humane Society, hundreds of animals have been saved annually, going on to productive, happy lives as guide dogs, while enriching the silent lives of their human companions.

We have the closeness of a loving friend, and the benefits that come when one's world is widened by awareness of the auditory stimuli around us. Though I cannot hear birds or thunder, the whirr of strong winds, the splash of jumping fish, because of Sheena I know they are there. I can travel almost anywhere, my ears trotting along by my side.

The incredible essence of the acceptance of a disability is perhaps its visible evidence. My dear friend Paula, for instance, is a beautiful, vocal, quick-witted presence, noticed first because of her wheelchair. We were teenagers, playing touch-football one day, when Paula fell down and could not get up, in the last polio epidemic before Sabin and Salk. Limits are set by visual identification. Here is a human being who has limits. We see a verbal, irascible, loving person who cannot walk. Paula's wheelchair is an arresting statement.

There is no visible manifestation of nonhearing. I look perfectly fine, and fortunately, I speak well, projecting my voice that I hear as a whisper in ways I have learned from others . . . there is no *visible* sign of my need, no odd inkling about my appearance (at first glance) that tells you I am unaware of rain pelting our roof, that the churning engines of a tug pushing two heavy-laden barges past the good ship *Bette Anne* escape my notice until the tug's wake sets us arock. However, there *are* two differences about me, unnoticed most of the time: I wear two high-powered hearing aids . . . and I am always accompanied by a dog.

For many years, as a librarian, I worked at a specialized job with visually and physically handicapped readers. How did some deaf people speak so beautifully? I asked them often, in curiosity and awe, yet still an intellectual inquiry inwardly absorbed. How could I really *know?*

Belief—empathy—knowing—evolve from a specialness of direct contact. Even so, understanding is conditional. How, all those years when I worked with handicapped people, could I really know the separateness, the scariness, the isolation that descends with the seeping away of sound?

With my Sheena I touch the world again, a world so taken for granted, the world of sound.

And I ask myself odd questions: Are the waves whipping the jetties soundless, if no one is nearby to hear them? The screech of the gulls, the song of the wind, the whirr of world lifeness . . . does it all really happen if we cannot hear it? Does the tree falling in the forest, far from the receptive ears of life awareness, make a sound?

I finally have the answer to that ancient puzzle . . .

6

"*The rain I am in is not like the rain of cities. It fills the woods with an immense and confused sound. It covers the flat roof of the cabin and its porch with insistent and controlled rhythms. And I listen, because it reminds me again and again that the whole world runs by rhythms I have not yet learned to recognize . . . It will talk as long as it wants, this rain. As long as it talks I am going to listen . . .*"

THOMAS MERTON,
Raids on the Unspeakable, 1966

The experiment began one hot humid afternoon in a sudden summer thunderstorm, some years ago. We sat in the cockpit of my home, the good ship *Bette Anne*, Elsa and I, and Sheena, my hearing guide dog. Several of the houseboat's resident cats lay sprawled under chairs, in dark corners, trying to escape the heat. I watched lightning flicker from afar, then nearer, dark thunder clouds building and scudding toward us out of the western sky. We waited, breathless, for that first whiff of wind, that rush of rain running down our faces, necks, arms. Only Sheena moved in the heavy heat, lifting her head quite often, placing a paw on my bare toes. She hears something, I thought . . . probably some fishing skiffs coming in, caught in the rain.

For it was raining now, where the harbor opens to the Sound. We could see the wall of water moving, slanted sharply, pushed by gusty breezes we ached to feel. Soon the trees on shore were sweeping sideways, the reed grass rippling, each gull claiming the top of a nearby marina piling, all facing in the same direction into the wind. "Amazing, isn't it," I said to my old friend, ". . . we really have not had a real thunderstorm in years . . . just these rain and lightning storms . . . "

Elsa stared at me for quite a while. The rain reached us, rushing through the open west side of the cockpit. Only the cats moved inside. The rain and wind were cool, caressing our skin, clearing our minds, carrying to us the collective scents of the sea. Elsa reached over to the cooler, refilling our vodka-and-tonics. "I propose a toast," she said slowly, ". . . to our friendship," adding, ". . . I suggest an experiment . . . a risk . . . a daring . . . it will test the strength of our friendship . . . but we must chance it . . . "

I waited.

"Hannah . . . dear friend . . . there is *always* thunder with lightning . . . "

A familiar fear furtive and frightening furrowed inside of me, became almost a physical pain. Of course there was no thunder.

I ran inside, rain dripping everywhere, pulling books from shelves. One dictionary stated: "thunder—a loud explosive, resounding noise produced by the explosive expansion of air heated by a lightning discharge . . . " Another book indicated all thunderstorms produce lightning and thunder. Still another described thunder as "a sound produced by lightning discharge . . . the reverberation . . . made by a sudden expansion in the air as the bolt of lightning passes through it . . . "

Apparently lightning did not happen by itself.

". . . So . . . it is really there." I was outside, the storm already abating, rain now falling lightly, the sky of late afternoon becoming the pale blue of early evening.

"Yes . . . Sheena was telling you for some time. I watched her . . . you must learn to listen to her, to all this . . . " Elsa waved an arm across our horizon.

When did I forget it was there—thunder? And why? And did it matter? What relevance to my life was it to know, as I do now, that I could estimate how far from me lightning is by counting the seconds between a slash of lightning and the thunder that would follow some moments later? Dividing that figure by five gives a rough gauge of the lightning's distance in miles (or dividing by three for the kilometer distance). Without immediate personal knowledge of thunder the distance of this elemental wonder becomes unimportant. Only lightning lights up my world, spectacular staging, seemingly close and live, measurements as afar from thinking as the thudding thunder I cannot hear.

"Shall we begin," Elsa was saying, "to awaken you to the world around you . . . ?"

And so the experiment began.

We met often, Elsa and I, to talk about the books we read, our creative endeavors—hers in the field of dance, mine in writing—and on every phase of life that crossed our thinking. We thought we knew each other well. We were to learn a lot about each other and ourselves in the next year.

We agreed the experiment would be conducted on several levels. Elsa, from that moment, would begin to actively "listen," always thinking, wherever she was, "What do I hear? Would Hannah hear this if she were here?"

When we were together she would ask me what around us had sound connected to it. One night in a restaurant I pointed to the piano, then gasped with shock. Someone was playing. I could not hear it. An immense sadness caught hold of me. Elsa did not say anything. We talked about the music I used to play when I had my piano. She mentioned the names of each piece played during our dinner. I began to enjoy the mental images of where my fingers would be on the keys. Next time we sat closer to the piano so I could watch the pianist's fingers.

Other times I would look around, wherever we were, saying there must be sound as the waves hit the shore; the wind, strong that day, could surely be heard, or perhaps I would see a powerboat skimming the bay, or a seaplane lifting into the air. Elsa would tell me what she was hearing. It could be announcements from the loudspeaker of the marina just beyond us. It could be the hiss of the mute swans, or the awful squawk of a night heron. It could be the practicing of another liveaboard's saxophone. (I began to discover there were some advantages to not hearing.)

We agreed she would work with me training my new hearing guide dog, my rambunctious, curious, alert, independent Sheena. Though Sheena came to me with exceptional skills I was often careless about reinforcing her training. Sheena was continually informing me about sound around me. I often failed to listen.

And lastly, we agreed that whenever we were with other people Elsa would tell them about the experiment. We found mixed reactions. We wanted to encourage people to share their world of sound with me, to help in my reawakening. One night someone described a concert recently attended. The rendition of some Chopin nocturnes had been exquisite. "Which ones were played?" I asked quickly.

"Oh ... well ... you wouldn't know what I meant anyway ... " An assumption. How could I know music if I cannot hear most of it?

"Tell me," I repeated. "I can still play all those nocturnes from memory ... I know their different feelings ... " Yes, I was getting braver.

It was with great hesitancy that other people began to participate in the experiment. We did not deny, Elsa and I, that there were moments of great stress. I was often overwhelmed with the onslaught of what I did not know was happening in my immediate surroundings. But I depended on Elsa's unswerving honesty and her caring demonstrated in her strictness to our purpose (a dancer's discipline) to be there even when I retreated, something I did often.

The experiment ended one day when Elsa realized I was listening on my own, not likely to be unaware anymore. At a party I see someone strike a match. There is sound with that. A canoe paddles by . . . sound there too. A loose halyard is flying back and forth against a mast . . . there is an old clinking sound reverberating somewhere in memory. I am washing dishes . . . water is splashing in the sink. Somewhere I remember there is sound to running water.

The day the experiment ended a little more than a year after it began was hot and muggy. Several guests were lounging in the cockpit of the *Bette Anne*, some occasionally turning a hose over their heads to cool off, all of us watching approaching thunderheads.

Too many voices at once confuse me. I cannot be certain what has been said, who has said it. I responded to a question with an answer that had nothing to do with the inquiry. "You haven't heard a thing I've said." My guest was annoyed.

I smiled, looking off at distant slashes of lightning, now cutting across a darkening sky. "Do you know," I said, suddenly aware that everyone was watching me, perhaps worried that I would be upset by the comment, ". . . do you know that there is always thunder after lightning . . . ?"

Of course, the experiment never ended. It is a continuous elliptic in the day-night-day cycle of my life. I cannot look at anything, be anywhere, without thinking, Does *this* have sound, vibration, swish in the swing of life? My hands on my typewriter *feel* the hum of my thoughts before they appear on the paper before me. And so much of what I have written since the inception of the experiment reflects an enlarged view of things, despite the diminishing of an important life dimension . . . sound.

Several weeks after the onset of the experiment a major New York newspaper flew me to the side of a mountain in the hills of New Hampshire. I who trip over pebbles was left at a campsite along the Appalachian Trail. I was writing a story about Mike Conway, a young blind man who was walking 1,000 miles in 100 days with his guide dog Tessy and a sighted friend. He wanted to raise money for the training of a guide dog like his own, so much did Tessy mean to his life. It was day number fifty on the walk. The rewards along the way had been many for the ardent hiker who could no longer see.

I came home, easily writing most of the article, but I could not finish it. I remembered day fifty in those blue-green rolling hills. I remembered the clouds whirling in wisps high overhead. I remembered the earth smells of the forest. But there was something I could not remember.

That evening I awoke in the moonlit stillness of the hot night. I climbed out onto the deck of the houseboat. Under a million stars I watched two egrets feeding at the tideline. A few mallards glided near them, hushed in the heavy air. A single gull, unmoving, did not seem real, seemed part of the rock on which it perched. In the morning the gull would screech, the mallards croak hoarsely, the egrets squawk low as they shuffled about for food.

Suddenly, I knew what I could not remember. Walking on day fifty in those wooded hills there must have been soft rustlings of wildlife, crunching of old leaves beneath our feet. Where were those fine woodland singers, that furtive forest creature, the thrush, where were those flute-like trills? Where was the whistle of the meadowlark, the lispy rough notes of the vireo, the bustling chirps of starlings and sparrows? And as I left, in the crimson-skied evening, there must have been a whippoorwill calling.

Sitting in the night with the egrets I was joined by Sheena, my gift from the Guide Dog Foundation. She curled in an orange heap against my leg, always moving to me, always with me. It was the silence I did not want to remember. There were birds in those mountains on day fifty. I just could not hear them though memory of their voices stayed with me.

Sheena lifted her head, licked my nose, placed a paw on my knee. She was watching someone, something behind me. She was telling me, in our special language, that someone, something was there, someone else awake at this hour, watching our wildlife with us. I patted Sheena's head and thanked her, this gift that is my ears. I thought about Mike and Tessy somewhere on the mountain. Though missing a sense, our guide dogs gave us a way of perceiving the world, enabling us to touch the world again, a world so taken for granted, the world of sight and sound.

At that midnight moment, under those thundering stars that I knew were there too, over that distant mountain, I felt incredibly close to Mike Conway.

"*. . . sound wends its way into the very core of our being. The proof is that traces of it remain hooked, like ragged tatters, in the soul's inward recesses. That is why, unexpectedly, we may hear sounds that no one perceives . . . let the sensory stimuli cease, as in deafness, or the attention be flattened, as in depression, and the sound memories will reemerge, like stubborn weeds, into the sunlight of conscious awareness.*"

F. GONZALEZ-CRUSSI,
The Five Senses, 1989

 A herd of a hundred elephants is grazing in grasslands, each occasionally lifting a huge heavy head from the vegetation of the veld to poke in a nearby dry riverbed for water which may not be too far below the surface. The elephants have been searching for an adequate watering hole for days. Suddenly, simultaneously, they are still, stiffened, raising great heads high in the African silence, spreading ears, in utter stillness scanning the atmosphere, motionless for as long as a minute. They are listening.

It is unheard of. They are thirsty, yet as one they turn from their feeding place released from synchronous "freezing" by a secret silent communication, speeding toward the source of a call that might have requested help, announced predators, declared with joy the finding of water.

The unhearable air vibrations of the elephant, sent out on infrasonic air waves below the level of human hearing, are messages of memory, elemental utterances of distress summoning aide, or impartings of vital information. Often these messages are the intense silent song of a female finally in estrus again after four years—two years of pregnancy and another two years of nursing her young one. Her singing sent across the miles expresses her urgent imperative need to wandering males, for her time of fertility will be a scant two days. On soundless infrasonic currents she sends her supplicant sequence of rising and falling rumbles, a song always the same, the mating call of the female elephant planted in memory.

Memory, Aristotle said, plays an important part in how men live. "Experience," he stated in his philosophical writings, "comes into being from memory." Animals, too, he believed, live by the aid of memory, "but the race of men lives also by art and judgment."

Perhaps. Art and judgment evolve in each human being in varying degrees. The individual result of experience-applied-to-living is a capricious blend of knowledge, temperament, and physical and mental ability imbued by memory.

Thinking about elephants, the quirks of quiet thinking, the maze of memory brings to mind the tree falling in the forest, "the waves whipping the jetties . . . the screech of the gulls, the song of the wind, the whirr of world lifeness . . . does it all really happen if we cannot hear it . . . "

Sound exists, I decided long ago, whether or not *my* ears

tell me it is there. Or does it? Or was Thoreau right when he wrote in his journal, "it takes a man to make a room silent"?

In a dictionary of music I read, in the section on acoustics, that sound is a sensation, rather than a thing. Vibrations are set up by some agency—a piano, a person's vocal chords, a plunging airplane—into the surrounding atmosphere. The eardrum of a live creature becomes aware of a nervous disturbance, a quivering, a quickening distraction there which our brain calls "sound." Looked at this way, my musical compendium notes, "there is 'sound' only where there is an ear; a brass band of stone-deaf players (if the imagination can fly so high) in a deaf and dumb asylum where only the patients were present would produce no 'sound.' "

What about my tree falling in the forest? My waves, my wind, my whirring world? What about the synchronous streaming of several widely spaced herds of elephants to a jungle tryst, suddenly, simultaneously striding away from a watering hole or the succulent brush nearby, all converging, responding to some splendid silent command? Two kinds of thinking are happening here, one philosophic, one scientific. For many hearing impaired people they overlap, come together, the known of the one, the scientific, illuminating the other, the hard-to-grasp abstraction of the philosophic (does sound exist if an ear does not acknowledge it?). For the hearing impaired the boundaries of sound discernible to average human hearing have altered, narrowing the span of perception. We need to fathom, to grasp absolutes and abstractions. The range of human hearing is measured by the frequency of complete cycles of pure tones per second. One complete cycle per second is known as the hertz. A pure tone is an undulating movement of air oscillating at a fixed rate, short puffs, for instance, from one's mouth. Blowing ten puffs of air in a second would create a frequency of ten hertz.

The highest frequencies our ears are capable of perceiving vary from 16,000 to 20,000 hertz, depending on health and age; 20 hertz is about the lowest we can interpret as sound. Air pressure changes below that frequency are sensed as vibrations, felt intuitively rather than heard. Thus ten puffs from one's mouth per second—10 hertz—would be cast into silence. But try speeding those puffs up to twenty or thirty per second. The average person is aware of sound from 30 to 18,000 hertz. With the increase in puffs comes an increase in the frequency, the pulsing of the energy being transmitted. Those puffs close together at some point become audible sound.

Sound does not fall off a cliff at either end of the hertz scale but extends to highs—ultrasound, and to lows—infrasound, realms of hearing known to living creatures other than man. In ultimate highs, beyond our sensing, in the ether of the ultrasonic, bats send out messages through echolocation; shrews, some insects, porpoises communicate with their kind; and dogs respond to an ultrasonic whistle constructed by nineteenth-century scientist Sir Francis Galton for their ears alone, one emitting high notes to which dogs heed, perfectly clear to them but inaudible to human ears.

Overlapping some of our lowest audible tones and ranging below them lies the world of infrasound. Infrasound rumbles around us, a stirring of air or water generated by wind, thunder, earthquakes, ocean waves and severe forms of weather. In the deep tone cycles of infrasound crocodiles converse, whales whisper and sing to one another, and intimations of importance are exchanged by large exotic birds like the three-toed rhea and the flightless cassowary. And beyond that edge of human hearing, beyond the elephant's resounding roars, trumpets, growls, barks, snorts that are known to us, the infrasonic infusions of elephant message-rumbles resonate across miles with specific intent. "I repeatedly noticed," a researcher commented, "a palpable throbbing in the air like distant thunder, yet all around me was silent."

Elephants freeze in their tracks to listen. They listen to a language as ancient as their mammoth selves. Females seem to be more vocal, their calls not always sexual but often rich with family connections involving care of calves, baby-sitting, how far to wander with young ones, how long to rest when a calf needs napping. The separate-living male elephants listen as much for the societal needs of the roving female families as for their location and sexual state of availability.

The discovery of the elephant's infrasonic calls with their varied harmonic structure was "like suddenly finding a tribe with a hitherto unknown language," said one wildlife scientist. Low-frequency vocalizations, beyond human hearing, are thought to be a method of secret communication over short and long distances. A spot on the elephant's forehead flutters producing infrasonic vibrations in the frequency range of 14 to 24 hertz. Somewhere in the wild another elephant is listening, pausing on wide plains, immobile, mute-seeming, ears lifted, listening to a lyric long known. Elephants have long acknowledged the existence of the extended family. Perhaps not art—but surely judgment—is part of their moment-by-moment existence. Would Aristotle be dismayed, or unbelieving, to learn of the caring of elephants for their kind as revealed by electronic printouts that record their unheard language? Does "the race of men" live today by so near a commitment to kind?

My span of aural perception is small. Most of the audible world out there is ultra and infrasonic—beyond my immediate knowing. Descartes proposed reasoning supported by evidence to prove that nonhuman animals were inferior to human beings in understanding, awareness, thought. Ah—another exponent of art and judgment on the human level. Would he reconsider elephants ... or find a pedestal for hearing guide dogs like my Sheena who makes the far-ranges of hearing known to me without electronics?

I would hope so. She deserves one.

8

> *"I like to watch him . . . I know where he stands and where*
> *his voice goes on the rolling grasses and where the sun comes up on*
> *the land. There, at dawn, you can feel the silence. It is cold and*
> *clear and deep like water. It takes hold of you and will not*
> *let you go."*

N. SCOTT MOMADAY,
The Way to Rainy Mountain, 1969

 He sat on the top step of the companionway, blinking away rain dripping from the hood of his foul weather jacket, waiting for my full attention, smiling, musing abstractions appearing as creases above his eyes. "How can I tell you the sound of the foghorn . . . " he said, ". . . describe how I hear night rain on the deck, on the dock, on the melting ice . . . ?"

I touched his hand, a silent gesture to convey the wave of caring that came over me, an unspoken "thank you" for giving a piece of the soft evening to me . . . for reminding me of the forgotten part of it that was there, the part I cannot hear.

"You have just told me," I said, and he knew memory was struggling to some shadowy recess trying to remember a foghorn rising and receding on a reachable horizon, the dull drone of a deep sigh over invisible water, gentle and firm, a giant's voice guarding the near breakwater, reaching out from those rocks every seven seconds in an ascending arc, leaving only a mind echo.

He stood then at the foot of the stairs, the open hatch above his head letting in the rain, the remarkable sky. We had noticed it earlier, walking our dog. Clouds scudded swiftly, greys and lavenders disappearing in gathering night mist. Through the hatch I could see a ribbon of white curling in a light south wind, steam from the garbage-burning plant down the inlet, wispy then lost in a vanished fog-world.

"Maybe," he said, "the foghorn . . . a sound not unlike an open G string." He smiled, hopeful. I tried to recall the rich tone of a violin's lowest string unstopped by fingers, a plucked evocation of a rising and falling of vibrating air. Once I knew the foghorn, the G string.

"And the rain." He turned, sliding shut the hatch, slipping off the wet slicker, tossing it over a doortop to dry. "How can I describe how beautiful it is . . . "

"It is light," I say, almost to myself, "almost a whisper . . . sinking silently into the wood of the dock, perhaps plinking off our deck, merging into the melting ice . . . " I know the plinking on deck must be muted, faint, even restful, a surprise with the soft air of this mid-February evening. I know the rain. We have talked about rain before. It is the foghorn we have forgotten to remember.

The foghorn becomes a small miracle, then an infinite wonder as we try to make tangible its essence, its august statement, mournful and solemn: I am rocks, I am ship, I am presence, I am here with you though you cannot see me . . . and the sound becomes anthropomorphic . . . , as do many sounds, as we talk about them. They become alive to me in ways they never were when I could hear them.

"Tonight's rain," Harvey says to me, "is like this . . . " He brushes my face with light glancing kisses, lips just resting on cheeks, eyes, lips, then gone, leaving a moist sweetness. I know what rain is like tonight, a tenderness I can guess from walking in it, touching it, but now I think I know its other dimension, can almost "hear" its sound, tonight close to silence.

My world—the world I know—is hushed, quiescent, since a skiing accident more than twenty years ago. One morning the world was there, perceived as it was every other morning, without conscious thought about what I saw, what I heard. By evening of that day the world I knew had changed, one dimension of perception dimming, soon nearly disappearing, the colorful sequence of words and sounds eclipsed until, months later, I almost forgot those chromatic cadences had ever been there.

Almost.

Memory was there, waiting for me to prod it, poke at its intricate filing system, play with its stored reserve of subtleties. Memory was motionless holding its breath, waiting to be prompted, waiting for urgency to invoke recall, the remembrance of sound. Memory waited for me to use it. What I needed, though I did not know it yet, was to learn a new language, to limn the linguistics of visual and auditory cues that were everywhere, there for me but unnoticed, unseen, unheard. I needed to learn the language of listening.

Can there be such a thing—a listening language—a linguistic composite capturing the complexity of thought and quest, catching the nuances of conceptual thinking, of feeling, of mood that can be found in, say, the Italian language, the French, the Hebrew, or in Sign, that exquisite choreography of silent movement and expression and fluttering fingers?

Indeed, Sign *is* a listening language, depending on visual attention and interpretation, a means of linguistic communication with a structure comparable to written and spoken languages. The many sign languages, all with individual forms of grammar and sentence structure, some including gestures of hand, head, and body to articulate the intent of meaning, are as real living languages as any written or spoken cultural cumulation of verbal expression. The hearing impaired, the not-totally deaf who have once known hearing and speech, often incorporate if not the syntax, then some of the physical means used by sign languages to both impart and receive communication.

As an adult losing most of my hearing suddenly, a loss leaving me in a strange semi-silent place, was a state akin to being adrift in a fog where the edges of nearby land, other fogbound craft, are barely visible. You know something is there but definition is vague. Depth perception plays tricks with distance. You miss a lot, the fog hiding much in a moist mist, sometimes unexpectedly lifting, giving you a glimpse of something you cannot make out. No one knows you are lost for you look the same. You can speak clearly the language you have known for years, but now your own voice, the voices of others are muffled, muted, or not there at all. You are aware yet cut off, alone in a scary isolation. The world is running forward and you cannot keep up. That is what it is like to be severely hearing impaired.

Who teaches the language of listening, and can it be taught? Not at all surprising is that my first teacher was a dog, my devoted brindle boxer, the first to recognize that I needed other ears, for though memory was ready, willing, able to supply years of gathered information it needed to know where to focus its research. We are information collectors, though we may never think of ourselves that way. Everything we do and see and hear and read, all the people we meet, all the worlds we touch are recorded in the library stacks of our minds. So much is there waiting for the right buttons to be pressed. You notice this most in doing crossword puzzles, especially sitting down to one that looks impossible from the first. You get a letter here, a word there, then suddenly memory clicks. Of course! You knew that all along! Just needed a reminder, a jolt, a trigger to awaken the slumbering tidbit, stored there who knows when.

It is there, the world, its music, its noise, its voice. I am in touch with it through the ears of others and my own memory of what has sound attached to it. Two hearing aids make more words recognizable to me but hearing aids are limited (in this early stage of their evolution) in the magic they can perform. More than my hearing aids I need Harvey and Sheena, my sisters, my friends, all partners with me in listening.

"It's alarming . . . " Harvey murmurs, an inert form beside me, unmoving although he has a commuter train to catch to New York. I cannot hear the alarm, a modernness that more beeps than alarms, Harvey tells me. Memory has not stored the sound of beeping alarm clocks for me. They have come into the world after my deafness. So each morning when Harvey mutters "It's alarming" I think of the round white-faced clock with large black numbers that jangled me alive eons ago, always at an hour, it seemed, before I was ready to face the world. Harvey stretches, sits up, careful not to disturb the cat or two or three sharing our bed. I close my eyes against sound waves I know are present, happy they are hidden from me. My life is improved without alarm clocks. Alarms of the "alarming" kind, that is, those of strident sound, those of an insistent signal signifying morning, symbolic sonic statements spinning through the silence of sleep, violent disruptions of a natural kind of order. I have a different kind of awakening clock.

No mechanical messenger brings morning's coming to me. I have an alive alert attentive presence, rousing herself from her own repose to tell me night is leaving, that light is creeping over the eastern sky. Sheena, my canine ears, is trained among other things to be an alarm clock, to awaken without being alarming, to whisk me gently from the warmth of woolen blankets, wing me away from the weight of sleep.

Sheena knows our routine. She is stretched where she has been sleeping, on a small settee adjacent to our bed. She watches Harvey sleepily stumble by our coal stove to the beeping loran-alarm clock, watches him press a button erasing the sound for those who can hear it. Her ears, her eyes follow him. He has walked the four or five steps into our galley, filled the copper kettle with cold water. Sheena lifts an ear, an acknowledgment not only of the splash of water into the empty drum of the kettle, but also of the electrical hammer-like pounding of our water pump, a low guttural grinding of gears that accompanies the turning on of our faucets. If I am alert enough, watching her, struggling to stretch my eyelids against their slumbering intent, I will see the lift of her other ear. Harvey is grinding beans for our morning coffee. In my near-slumber, in the snug cocoon of my bed, half aware of beginning day, I am listening to morning, hearing it without sound, knowing it all by cues from listening ears, ears that are not my own.

I resist the moment of change from warmth to cold air. Harvey has not yet attacked the fire. No abrasiveness yet assails the dim light, the sound of shaking down the night's ashes, a sound I will know is there when I see him sitting on the step by the stove, shivering while he plays with the morning fire, coaxing it back to vibrant life. The fire, too, has rested through the night, burning low in the early hours, needing the alarm of a shake and fresh fuel. I do not move, buried beneath the covers to my nose, until my personal alarm clock rings.

She is silent, setting about her work with no jarring to the senses. I sometimes think my first sense of her is a seductive dream I am still part of. Sheena begins with the part of me nearest the edge of the bed . . . an arm draped over the side, an elbow jutting over her settee . . . or if I am too cuddled under, my nose, my cheek, my forehead. I feel a rough tongue, an insistent paw pressing a hip, a shoulder, my hair. She does this only for a moment, her whole self expectant, waiting, giving me time. She knows me.

". . . Hmmmm," I murmur, burrowing deeper under the blankets. Instantly Sheena is on the bed, a gentle but firm emphatic presence, two paws on my shoulders, a nose nuzzling my neck. "Get up," she is saying, "coffee is ready, morning is here, you love mornings . . ."

And I do. Love mornings, that is. I am always resistant to rising, yet happy to be up, eager to climb on deck even when freezing to watch the sun rise over the hills of Sea Cliff, over the hazy housetops of Glen Cove, over the incinerator stack not far from us at the head of the creek. Sheena is a superior alarm clock even if a silent one. She will not be ignored or turned off until obeyed. She persists, knowing I relish the early hours.

In the half-light, half-dark we sit in the enclosed cockpit of our home, the good ship *Haimish*, sipping strong coffee, a fresh-ground blend of espresso and French roast beans—the mixing, the smelling, the sipping all making a miracle of our mornings.

9

 It is late April and they are here every morning now, the ménage à trois (sometimes quatre ou cinq), mama resplendent in cinnamon and puce, ecru and umber (what the books so unimaginatively call mottled brown). She waits for me on the substructure of the dock to which our floating home is tied, sitting on beginning gatherings of grass and twigs and down carefully placed on the boards she has nested on for years. Her drake pulses a shiny green-purplish head a few feet from my window, Broken Wing and other challenging rogues seemingly still in a respectfully-distanced arc behind him. Not for long.

My morning appearance, when it happens, initiates movement. In my old bathrobe, still foggy with sleep, I am light-years away from them in garb and attention. My left hand reaches for the mug of steaming black coffee Harvey places before me. My right hand automatically unlatches the window, pushing it open. I have not called to them as I will later in the day when I feel more alive. I have just appeared at the window's edge. Only air and water are between us. Even as I reach to the shelf behind me for the loaf of bread that is always there, a fluttering has begun. Mallards and geese swim toward me from the opposite shore of the creek, a gentle wake rippling behind each bird. Black-headed gulls hover low overhead, waiting to dive, to pluck a chunk of whole wheat from the water. And papa duck lowers his head, flattens his wings tightly against himself, becomes a speeding brilliant bullet aiming himself at the rogues who scatter and return. "Movement," professed Martha Graham, "is the one speech which cannot lie."

Papa mallard treads water a few feet from me, glancing hither and yon protectively. No matter how many small chunks of bread I toss out he will not take a bite until mama begins to eat. I wait for her, tossing further to Broken Wing and the others. Mama does not like this, a swishing volcano-burst of energy from under the dock, vaulting the six or more feet from water surface to my eye level, white tail aquiver, flashing her dazzling blue speculum sides before set-tling in the water, rising once again, her whole self a vertical vibrating voice. Ah, yes. "A gesture does not exist alone in time."

Aristotle believed perception, sensing, and some under-

standing of the immediate environment were characteristic
of all animals and quite a few plants. Perceiving, he deduced,
caused a physiological change in the perceiver, became part
of memory; therefore biological studies, especially consider-
ations of the senses, could not be separated from study of
the mind. Last week, more than 2,000 years *après* Aristotle, I
read about a "new discovery": "Plant communities may be
abuzz with conversations no one can hear." My pansies and
petunias (and who knows what else) are staking out territory by underground signals, by "root communication." Oh,
dear. What are my dill and parsley and thyme saying to each
other? (She spends too much time at the typewriter, forget-
ting to water us!) Plants send out wordless messages through
their roots, chemical signals called alleopathy. Not so new.
In 1880 Charles Darwin wrote a book (*The Power and Movement of Plants*) describing his reflections and observations of
plant tendrils, their selective responses to stimuli, their elab-
orate movements that evince remarkable sensitivity to the
provocations around them.

So it is. Communication is everywhere. A root wiggles,
saying, this is *my* place. Mama mallard ejects herself skyward
to my eye level, saying, breakfast! (or lunch, or snack, or
dinner, as the case may be). As soon as she begins to munch
papa may take a nibble, all the while wary of predators who
want both breakfast and mama duck. He nibbles, then
swivels, hunching down, zooming like a high-speed motor-
boat, a missile aimed first at Broken Wing (who can easily
outdistance him . . . he's the fastest duck on the creek), then
at the other rogue ducks. While he scoots at the others, Bro-

ken Wing takes a momentary sexual interlude atop mama. Breakfast.

Silent signaling is not just reserved for breakfast. An egg lingering lethargically somewhere along the human female reproductive system can, at any time of day or night, according to recent research, exhibit selectivity, emitting a chemical lure, beckoning to particular potential partners among the perhaps 280 million sperm swimming her way from one ejaculation. Endocrinologists are at work trying to characterize and isolate the attractant.

Will the creation of a child cease to be, sometime in the future, a random miracle? Will there be any mysteries left? Is the best communication silent, wordless?

Could be. Nevertheless, I turn to Harvey, push aside my coffee, the toast and jam, use words. Let's have breakfast . . .

They filled the early morning sky, a long arcing skein, their honking a musical conversation competing with the whistle of the high west wind of earliest day. Following their leader in quivering vee-formation they clung to the coast of the harbor, easing down, veering left at the creek, a sinuous ribbon-stream swaying into the sunrise shadows, circling mud-flats, skidding to splashdown on the surface of the creek in the lee of the land. There were well over 100 of them.

More remarkable than their guided direction, their secret communication that led them to soar, descend, slip to land in one breathless choreographed motion, was what they did next. With the same single-minded action that brought them within fifty feet of my floating home, they turned from the mudflats on the opposite shore, necks pulsing forward and back, propelling themselves across the creek. There was nothing random or hesitant heralding the manner of their approach. I watched them draw close, sipping my first morning cup of steaming black coffee, sitting on a deck still damp with the dew of dawn.

They did not draw near in an accidental pattern, but swam into a U-shaped form flanked on the huge outer rim by the largest, the fathers, the grandfathers, the uncles, tightly together, herding before them into another grand inner arc the grandmothers, the mothers, the aunts. In the center-front, protected, closest to me were the goslings of various sizes, all new to the world by only weeks.

Some of them must have been here before, must have known I would feed them, toss out broken-off bits of bread, whole wheat and pumpernickel, carefully thrown close within reach so they could grasp it before the scavenging gulls. Those few had communicated their news to the others, and now I had parents and babies, uncountable generations, an extended family of Canada geese encircling my home, expectant, extravagantly expressing the needs of their morning—breakfast.

I tossed out pieces of bread. The female geese pushed the young ones in to feed first, snatching a crust for themselves only when the babies were eating and the morsel threatened to disappear with a diving gull. The adult geese did not aggressively begin to feed until the children had eaten. This did not occur quietly, but with much vociferous commenting, and moments of chastising, with sharp pecks, to adolescents that tried to eat before the youngest were satisfied. Not so astonishing. The elders spoke, directed, disciplined. The flock listened. They had language.

Were my gregarious Canada geese wintering in these waters from Alaska, the Aleutians, the arctic Baffin Island? Had they flown from the northernmost reaches of Canada? Or were they part of the thousands-fold flock that makes Long Island its year-round home, no longer migratory, finding here on this island, with its parks and fields, golf courses, and large lawns, endless foraging, feeding, grazing grounds, an ideal island with short flights to miles of inlets and harbors to roost upon, with waterside nearby nesting grounds of tall grass and green moss? Had a few nested this year or last in an abandoned osprey nest, as Canada geese sometimes do, in the trees across the creek? Beyond the spicebush and arrowwood shrubs at the edge of wet thickets, above the low-lying marshes along the creek and sandy stretches of the harbor, I have watched their aerial formations all through any year. From the shallows and shore grasses they take off and land, long black necks and heads extended, white chinstraps striking and jaunty.

On this morning they stayed for an hour, fending off mallards and terns and the ever-present gulls. Then, alerted by a vocal signal, some specific statement from amidst the babble, they turned, swimming out of the creek, suddenly a soaring flock in flight, lifting over the trees on the far side of the creek, careening in careful close formation to another cove, honks rolling and deep, distinctly directing, their language.

"You must watch her," Elsa said to me eleven years ago, when Sheena became part of my life. "Watch the shape of each movement, how much effort is involved. Effort shape," Elsa said, leading Sheena in a mad-paced series of twirling leaps and jumps around her studio, "is the action, attempted endeavor [effort] that takes place in energy." Elsa recognized that although Sheena came to me superbly trained, she would be always adding to her canine nonverbal vocabulary. To become half of a successful team I must advert to every subtle stir of her silent silhouette.

My perceptions sharpened quickly. Elsa saw to that. Elsa, a dancer trained at George Balanchine's School of American Ballet, made nonverbal communication clear to me by teaching Sheena to dance, sometimes on point (a slight leap of the imagination). To this day (oddly—poor publicity, I suppose) Sheena is Elsa's only four-footed student.

Anyone who has ever lived with animals is aware of unspoken indications of mood. What I knew from living with a continually changing population of dogs and cats (and uninvited, yet resident mice, spiders, ants) was not superficial. It was just not enough. Much of my understanding of the fluctuating feelings of my creatures depended on sound. Now sound had escaped me, still there but elusive, beyond my knowing. I needed to hone visual skills. I needed to really begin to see.

I watched her dance. Hardly Balanchine material, but

then Elsa had worked miracles before. Our lessons were unscheduled, impromptu visitations at Elsa's studio when a class was in session. Sheena and I would climb the stairs, Sheena pausing midway, looking at me, her right ear lifted straight up, her head tilted sideways to the left, glancing upward, then at me, then upward again. After a while I knew this meant music. Elsa's class was practicing enchainements or classical ballet variations, watching form and stance in the mirrored wall opposite the studio entrance.

I never think of Sheena's lack of oral communication in our life together. (Her high sharp barks, her low guttural growls, are there for anyone else.) I am instead amazed by her ears that not only take in and translate sound for me but also seem to have a life of their own. Darwin discussed this at length in *The Expression of the Emotions in Man and Animals.* "The ears," he wrote, "through their movements are highly expressive in many animals; but in some, such as man, the higher apes, and many ruminants, they fail in this respect. A slight difference in position serves to express in the plainest manner a different state of mind, as we may daily see in the dog." This is clear in Sheena's manner of telling me her water bowl is empty. She rushes to me with both ears pointed high, her signal for alarm, then drops her ears flat against her head, glances at the bowl which she has turned upside down, then runs to it, pushing it with an annoyed paw, rushing back to me, ears still plastered against her collie-like skull.

At Elsa's doorway, Sheena pauses an infinitesimal moment. I drop her leash. All grace is lost as she plunges toward Elsa, a tremolo rush of orange skidding to stillness at Elsa's toes, obeying Elsa's signal to her—a lifted hand, pointed finger raised, quickly lowered—meaning "Sit." Just as swiftly Elsa raises an arched arm, hand bent downward at the wrist, moving one finger in a continuing upward spiral. Sheena swivels on hind legs in a remarkably unBalanchine attempt at a pirouette.

Eleven years later. Sheena is not a dancer. And yes, she is, in the sense that she and I have learned that movement, overt signs of physical expression, are indicative of more than the mere action; movement concerns the psyche as well, illustrates and conveys feeling, thinking. Effort shape comes to mean the outer visualization of an inner surge, manifest. What is necessary for the observer is acute consideration of the motion performed. Ann Hutchinson, a Labanotationist skilled in the system of recording movement in Dance, defined such observation (*Labanotation: The System for Recording Movement*, 1970): "Behind each motion lies the inner originating impulse to which we give the name effort . . . Every action, from a tiny shiver to a jumping out of the way of an oncoming car, originates in some effort by the individual. In daily life, we complete our various jobs and express ourselves in various ways through a series of effort patterns."

I watch her dance. No plie, no pas de cheval, no grand leap can say more than the intricacies of Sheena's daily sign-dances to me. Again I think of Martha Graham: "The dance must be strong. All that is important is this one moment in movement. Make the moment vital and worth living. Do not let it slip away unnoticed and unused."

I watch her dance. Walk. Run. Speak to me in her sign-movement way, exploring with intelligence, conveying with care, our world. And I am struck, feeling her napping weight across my toes this moment as I sit at my typewriter. She is twelve years old, perchance more. A senior citizen of dogdom. I reach down, stroking her rugged flank, reassuring myself of her presence. She rolls over on her back, lifting paws.

Of course. She prefers belly rubs.

10

"He knew language in a way that I never will. He danced it
from his soul. To him language was a mantle, wearable. To
Momma, language was tenderness, a protective touch, a means to
tell me her stories, to hold me close to her life. And together, they
brought me to a language beyond signed words."

RUTH SIDRANSKY,

In Silence, 1990

 A hand hovers hesitantly before my face, fingers
fanning its far reaches before resting on my cheeks,
my neck, my vocal cords, a thumb light, listening
on my lips. It is the signal for me to begin our conversation.
Receptive now to every flickering vibration, motion, breath,
he smiles.

We speak to each other. Our random thoughts and feelings are perceived by this man through his fingertips; by me,
by watching his lips. He cannot see me. He cannot hear me.
Deaf and blind, he interprets speech through vibrations and
lip movements, aware through sensory messages of the subtle nuances occurring in verbal exchange. He is listening.

His voice is heard by me by tones still taken in by my inner ear, vague cadences caught, mute and muffled as they are, and by concentration on the vivid expressions of his face, his lips. We listen to each other, a conversation almost totally dependent on visual and tactile cues.

Dr. Robert J. Smithdas, director of the Helen Keller National Center for Deaf-Blind Youths and Adults, is fluent in several "languages." He is using three almost simultaneously at this moment: the Tadoma method of speech communication—the reading of vibrations of a voice with the fingers (could even be toes—a method developed by a teacher trying to convey communication skills to two deaf-blind students, Tad and Oma) wherein the person without sight and sound sensation sharpens other perceptions by the sense of touch—the position of the tongue, the movements of cheek hollows, the windpipe's airflow, all the large and small, swift or slow movements of muscles occurring with articulation; Bob is also using fingerspelling, the one-hand manual alphabet that relays words and letters—his left hand rests atop his secretary's hand, receiving by touch a series of finger and knuckle positions conveying the key words I am uttering. And third, Bob, though he cannot hear his own voice, is using speech. He is a sought-after lecturer astonishing audiences with his resonant voice, his varied vocabulary, his irrepressible humor. Watching him, listening to him, it is easy to forget the separateness of his world.

With a laugh he is quick to remind you. Once years ago I asked him how he learned to speak so well. Steadfastly, he said, he practiced articulation and deliverance with a friend, a blind opera singer. He remembers his first speaking engagement, the warm response of the audience, the loud applause he "heard"—vibrations beneath his feet. He remembers the sound ebbing even as someone fingerspelled into his hand a bit of advice: next time it might be interesting to face the audience.

Bob's conversation is filled with sensory images: "I had been playing by myself . . . chasing June bugs and butterflies," he mused, remembering the day at the age of five when he became ill with spinal meningitis. "I recall to this hour the large grey cat with yellow eyes . . . stretched out lazily on a porch across the street . . . Mother called me for lunch . . . hands on hips. She wore a bright print dress, her brown hair swept backward over her head." Three months later he recalls "trying to erase the film of drowsiness that clung to me like a mist. The darkness was neither black nor grey, but a thick muddy fog . . . " His own voice had become a babbling sound. He could not understand it, soon would not hear it at all. And he was blind.

Later, after a tour of the Helen Keller Center, I walk by myself through the halls. There are different colors at every intersection, the walls different textures. I close my eyes, walking slowly, fingers following the finite reaches of each texture, finding then another, feet feeling changes when one kind of tile changes to another, physically absorbing the impact of this special place. It is peaceful. It is beautiful, wholly uninstitutional. The outer grounds too are abloom with texture and color. I remember a section of Bob's autobiography, *Life at My Fingertips*, describing his first few months at Perkins Institute in

Massachusetts: "I became familiar with the grounds . . . It had been a principle with the founders of Perkins that the unseeing and unhearing should live in an aesthetically inspiring environment, for beauty has its own channels of communication, even when the senses are deficient . . . the old chestnut in front of Tompkins Hall broke into blossom, its wonderfully flowering branches overhanging the low wall that ran along the campus . . . when I walked along the flagstone paths of the herb garden my footsteps crushed leaves of thyme and sorrel, sending up a curtain of tart, mingled fragrances that hung like a giant censer in the sunlit air . . . and . . . I grew especially fond of a magnolia tree in the director's garden."

I opened my eyes and turned off my hearing aids. Morning sun lit an empty classroom looking out on a small garden. The room was long, an open door at either end. I sat down at a desk, my back to both doors, gazing out at the garden, taking notes on the morning.

I do not know how long I was there. Or how long they were there. It was when I dropped my pencil, watched it roll under another desk, reached for it, glancing up toward the door at the far end of the room that I saw them, talking to each other, each with fingers on the other's lips, free hands folded under and over each other's in fingerspelling, the sightless eyes of each gazing at some inner vision off in space, yet entirely together. I was breathless. It was beautiful. Bob Smithdas and his deaf-blind wife Michelle, a teacher at the Center, catching a private moment together.

And they did not know I was there.

I was the tree falling in the forest.

11

"... the postlingually deaf, who stay in the world of speech—
achieve some heightening of visual sensibility."

OLIVER SACKS,
Seeing Voices: A Journey into the World of the Deaf, 1989

"I do not notice more but notice differently."

DAVID WRIGHT,
Deafness, 1969

 I call him Elijah, now, although I have seen him
before, always at the edge of evening, easing out of
the creek-side shadows suddenly, and as suddenly
gone. He is not, I know, a reincarnation of the ninth century
B.C. Israeli prophet who wanders the earth heralding hospi-
tality and, as legend has it, assuaging immutable moments in
families when tensions test ties between fathers and sons,
daughters and mothers. Or is he? I named him Elijah last
April in the twilight hours of our Passover seder, at the
moment we opened the houseboat door, traditionally welcoming in that invisible patriarchal wanderer. At that
moment an auburn fluff appeared in the shadows of the
low-tide mudflats across the creek.

A hush fell over the ten at our white-clothed table, our best goblet in the center by tradition filled with a quaff of wine for the thirsty traveling prophet. We watched the dog-like head, muzzle tilted downward over a whitish throat and belly, ears pricked upward, walking slowly, almost cat-like, along the rising reedgrass. He paused, stilled to the white tip of his tail, the black patches on his shoulders stiffened, sniffing the wind, considering ordinary rustlings of frogs and flies, snakes, passerine birds, and his favorite, water rats.

An egret rose off the water capturing us. Right then, my frequent nocturnal visitor, red fox, was gone. And the goblet glistening for Elijah was empty.

Creatures of night negate the void aspect of darkness, discovering their world through wild sensation, discerning in dense lightlessness friend, enemy, prey. Nocturnal creatures are rarely deficient in sight, and often gifted with a keen sense of smell. However, it is with reliance on their sensing of sound that they slink through the darkened hours.

Red fox forages for food as day disappears, stalking prey for his pups hidden in a burrow midst the grove of trees across the creek from where I am typing. A spider stilled on symmetrically-spun strands of sticky silk, or maybe hanging from a new-woven thread, listens for a whir of wings, an insect en route to her fine filamental web. And somewhere on a western desert a kangaroo rat springs to safety at the moment a rattlesnake strikes, alerted in an instant to danger by light music that is the sound of survival, the sound of the rattlesnake's scales slipping over sand. (Understandably the snake is bereft losing such a succulent supper . . . such a tasty source of protein lost! Many a seaman has been saved from scurvy by a hearty rat stew, recommended not only by Magellan's crew but by more recent adventurers sailing to the arctic on the exploration ship *Advance*. Napoleon, too, on his exile island, partook of the local cuisine, reflecting " . . . a man's palate can, in time, become accustomed to anything . . . ")

Here in my northeast, far from desert creatures yet close to the coastal wild, I know a barn owl obscured in a hollow tree or in a crevice in creek rocks is listening for the patter of field mice and shrews, vaulting quick ears at voles and other small rodents, at rabbits and rats, flashing a talon at fireflies and frogs, at bats. And bats sleep until sunset, settling solitary or in clusters upside down in attics or trees or caves or abandoned structures such as the forsaken half-built spectral condos next to my red fox's nightly haunts, wakening to dip through the dark eavesdropping, emitting short supersonic bursts of shrieking sound we cannot hear.

Attentive after the lessening, the leaving of light, creatures of night listen in an unilluminated world, yet a world "seen" by them nevertheless. How does *Myotis lucifugus* plunge through the creekside woodland in unerring foraging flight snapping up midges and moths, caddisflies, crickets, lacewings, an occasional wonderful katydid? And all on the wing, the prey flicked from the air by the little brown bat's wingtip into the membrane between his legs that forms a convenient pouch, quickly lifted and tossed into his mouth. He is good at this, his foraging behavior not inherent, but learned, a listening skill. He is two years old, has come to know the rare gift of his built-in aerial hunting system—echolocation—a strategy of sensory feedback that grants him a hearty meal each night, that enables him to detect a near object as fine as a human hair. Echo-receiving for food finding and orientation is used by other living creatures—whales, seals, sea lions, dolphins, porpoises, many insects and some nocturnal birds—sonic systems that can sway the survival/death balance of life in the wild, all less evolved than that possessed by the world's millions of bats in their near 1,000 species. *Myotis* could conceivably live thirty years if he foregoes lovely katydids when his personal sonar system tells him to listen, that predators—an owl, a snake, a racoon—are waiting for a katydid to divert him.

My *Myotis* listens carefully to echoes in the air. Nightly he forages near and far, could be well over one hundred miles from the rafter he calls home, hunting mostly for nocturnal moths, his major prey, his extraordinary external ears, set farther apart and more mobile than most mammals, often mammoth for his size, sometimes folded or fanning out in all directions, detecting echo data from the several kinds of sounds he has sent out: buzzes and shrill cries within the perceptible hearing range of humans; an almost audible swift click; and his ultimate weapon, his ultrasonic cry. Flying low *Myotis*'s pulsations point out to him a floating log, a leaping frog, a bluefish lifting clear out of the creek catching insects and small surface-water fishlets. It is gourmet dining tonight.

Myotis's percussive ultrasonic clicks, short wavelength cries, return to him with an acoustical map of any live creature or thing in his path. With ease he evades obstacles, with utter preciseness aiming unerringly at insects of the evening, hoping for the not ordinary. Tonight it happens.

Alert and hungry he fills his small stomach in minutes, consuming katydids in their original state, not once considering Aristophanes' suggestion for preparation. They are excellent, noted the fourth-century B.C. Athenian, when roasted with a dash of pepper and aromatic vinegar ... a singular recycling of self to imagine. Bat guano is harvested to fertilize, among other things, nearly one third the world production of black pepper.

The Pterodactyl House looms over the point of land where the creek runs into the harbor, its many-gabled eaves forming multi-triangles on every side. Rangly brush grows wild around the half-finished haunting grey structure intended as the office for the half-begun condos. Great gaping odd-shaped windows bare broad-beamed rafters in its stark unfinished shell, daring drifting clouds to rush through with the whistling wind, with the darting barn swallows, past *Myotis* and his family dangling in the diurnal mode of bats, upside down, sleeping.

Myotis's kin have hung around here for years while the property rests in bankruptcy. Gulls, great blue herons, cormorants perch on its many roof angles. Named by the harbormaster "because it looks like something a pterodactyl would land on," it is a fitting home for bats with all the off-beat charm of an attic, a tree hollow, a belfry, a cave. And too, there are similarities in the visual perception of pterodactyls, the extinct flying reptiles, and bats, the only mammal capable of sustained flight, in their thin-membraned wings supported by an outstretched elongated digit. Other than wing-likeness and evolutionary ties there is little to connect the odd bird of over 135 million years ago with *Myotis* sleeping in a nearby rafter.

It is dusk. It is warm. Insects are plaguing the twilight hours of humans along the waterfront. For weeks evening meals have consisted of gnats, midges, horseflies. Tonight it sounds like mosquitoes. *Myotis* does not have to turn on his sonar echolocation system—one far more sophisticated than any yet devised by man—to know what kind of meal is out there. Noisy insects like mosquitoes and flies announce their presence to him by the particular sound of their wingbeats.

A yellow butterfly (twelve to eighteen beats per second) flits through the Pterodactyl's open windows. *Myotis,* still lethargic, misses him as he drops off his rafter. Gliding out a window into the evening shadows he knows instantly who is out there: some dragonflies wingbeating at a languid 20 to 30 beats a second, quite a few sizable moths noisier at a 50 to 70 rate, millions of midges at a snappy 1,000, and yes, delectable mosquitoes at a more leisurely beat of up to 600.

Long bones of his fingers stretched inside the membrane-wing seem like umbrella spokes. He sweeps them out, a small monkey-like head with two oversized ears peering out in between, skimming the shoal waters, listening even as he emits short shrill squeaks, using his larynx inside his vocal cords in much the same manner as do humans, piercing sounds unheard by the easy fishermen trawling in the creek for bait. The ultrasonic sounds produced by bats have frequencies of 40,000 to 100,000 vibrations per second—far above the threshold of 20,000—the very best of human hearing. Fortuitously, *Myotis* does not hear the deafening rending of the air as he sends out his strident high-pitched shrieks. His hearing mechanism, formed much like the human ear, would be deafened or irreparably damaged if exposed to such a noise level (sounds as intense as a propeller-driven aircraft at close range, or the almost-felt impact of nearby thunder), so at the moment he utters his ultrasonic cries a small middle ear muscle, provided by nature in one of the extraordinary processes of evolution, temporarily shuts off his hearing. Almost instantly his ear becomes functional again, allowing him to hear and react to echoes.

The keen hearing of *Myotis* picks up the echoes of his sound signals as they bounce off a moth, a mosquito, a frog, a tree limb, a leaf floating on the water. Born knowing that sound travels almost a quarter of a mile per second through air, *Myotis* considers and classifies echoes and their distance, listening to time lags between his shrieks and the returning echoes, slowly altering his flight direction, turning his head, collecting information that will pinpoint his target's location. A bat's auditory system is complex, enabling him to consider an echo's loudness, how long it took to reach him. The echoes tell him how far or near his dinner is. His echolocation system is so exact he can detect and pounce on a midge, perhaps a mere fraction of an inch long, from six feet away in total darkness. His sonar tells him not only where his next snack is located but the speed at which it is traveling, if the echoing object is an appropriate size for him to ingest. I often wish *Myotis* would hover around my craft on a hot evening when I am serving dinner. I know he can take in up to 3,000 mosquitoes a night despite his small size. He is a wanted but elusive guest as I dream of scratchless bug-free twilight summer hours.

A Xerox photograph of *Rhinopoma microphyllum*, a mouse-tailed bat (I have been calling her Phyllis), has been tacked to a wall by my typewriter for months, before and during my thinking about bats. Poor Phyllis is exposed in unseemly fashion, her small feet widespread, long tail dangling and curled between, her wonderful armbones and long fingers extended straight out holding her scalloped wing membrane. Worst of all each part of her is numbered, an ultimate intrusion by human scientific study defining the anatomy of a bat. She looks not quite like a bird or a mouse, more like my seven-week-old kitten who likes to sleep on her back. She looks so human.

I have taken her down, cut off the numbers, rehung her properly—upside down—facing the Pterodactyl House and her cousins only seconds away.

Listening—how live creatures perceive sound, pursue communication through other than written language—has not always been a popular scientific pursuit. I am not sure it is now, confused as it is with other directions, the "teaching" of listening as learned psychological behavior, or as a business/sales tool. Is spontaneity lost? I love reading about Abbé Lazzaro Spallanzani in his laboratory at the University of Pavia, in Italy in 1793, watching (I picture him puffing on his pipe) flying animals soar through the scrupulous sanctity of his scientific chambers. In the dark, when he extinguished his candles, his owls crashed into walls. His bats seemed able to "see" in the dark. In a lightless room he stretched silken threads from ceiling to floor and at odd intervals. In utter dark his bats wove through his threads with ease. He concluded his bats had a sixth sense, a something that rendered them capable of navigation in the night. It would be over one hundred years—1908—before an American scientist would confirm Spallanzani's theory that perhaps bats navigate in the dark by listening.

It would be almost as long before recognition would come that deaf or hearing impaired people can "hear" in the light.

At this moment seven small sailing sloops are skimming by down the creek, each captained by one young adult and manned by five to six young persons (about eight to ten years old). A sailing school is teaching them the ways of the wind, the whims of the water. All week I have noticed their strict attention to the immediate—commendable—yet no one glanced up—breathless—as a great blue heron winged overhead inches above them minutes ago; no one glanced at the seventeen great egrets at the water's edge; no one looked at a mother mallard and her ten babies born yesterday, swimming mid-creek.

How will they know, these young sailors, that there is more to sailing, to living, than touch-guiding one's tiller? In the pursuit of one skill or another will they glance around . . . listen . . . ?

It is nearly dawn. *Myotis* is pleasantly tired, lifting languid wings, then enfolding them close to him again, striking the soft summer air with a last few clamorous cries. Eating is work for my little brown bat. All night he has been performing skillful technical mathematical measurements, computing distances between himself and returning echoes, increasing the rapidity of his calls when he senses a target is a delectable morsel. The energy of the sonar pulse emitted by *Myotis* has been measured as twenty times the sound energy engendered by a pneumatic drill shattering city pavement heard at close range. An article in *Geo* magazine noted that "were these sounds not emitted at a frequency too high for us to hear, the night would bring with it an indescribable racket, sounding as though hundreds of high-speed motorboats were criss-crossing over our heads all night long."

Myotis becomes still for a moment, hanging invisible in the shadowy limbs halfway up the ninety-foot tulip tree across the creek. Two differing echoes have caught his concentration in his short-range acoustical world. One is large and farther away, the other minute-size and near, moving closer.

He offers to the air long bursts of sound sensing a longed-for unexpected dessert to his night-long meal, a golden-eyed lacewing. Did the Austrian mathematician and physicist of the early 1800s, Christian Johann Doppler, ever surmise or imagine that a little brown bat hanging from a tree on Glen Cove Creek in 1990 would be using the principle for which he is known, the Doppler shift, to top off an evening repast? The Doppler shift—the relationship between speed direction and frequency (of light, radio, sound wave sources)—occurs all the time. As the source and the listener draw close the waves crunch up, seem higher in pitch; if the space between listener and wave source widens, the waves spread out, seem lower in tone. The changing distance, Doppler declared, between a source of vibrations and an observer alters the true value of the sound or light wave as distance lengthens or lessens, an essential dynamic of echolocation.

In the near-dawn the golden-eyed lacewing flutters four similar wings, delicate almost transparent membranes, her network of veins sketched across them in a fine line drawing. She glistens in the growing light, undulating in the shadows, her eyes in their tiny head iridescent. Nocturnal, she has taken wing at twilight with fellow neuropterans, fluttering in the lamplight of shoreside homes, rainbow glints glancing off her gauze-like wings. A predator on the midnight shift, she is cannibalistically searching for other insects. It is incredible *Myotis* should notice her, pinpoint her exactly, for golden-eye is a mere wisp in the air, her body barely a twelfth of an inch long, her wing span not much more.

A searing soundless song sweeps through humid creek air, *Myotis*'s panting pulsings, unheard moving air bouncing off the delicate minute enchantment that is lacewing's tiny self.

An echo long-delayed would mean unbearable anticipation because of distance. *Myotis*, relieved, senses lacewing close. Returning echoes are received quickly. He increases crisp cries from 20 to 200 pulsations per second.

Myotis plucks golden-eye midair, throwing his legs forward, grasping the gliding lacewing in his membrane pouch, lazily flicking her into his mouth, all the while sending out strident cries to something else his echoes have reported, something nearly below him. He is far from alone in his sonar detections. Friends and family are all around him, all dining al fresco.

Aristotle predicted foul or fair weather by the number of bats he could see in the sky near sunset or just after. A chiroptera cloud means calm and mild for the next twenty-four hours, he wrote. A mere *Myotis* or two means the coming of stormy unsettled weather. He must have known bats are reluctant to leave their roosts in the disquiet of agitated air.

On another perspective, how can I begin to discredit the bad image of *Myotis* and his kin—noticed clearly, lately, when I am asked "What are you working on now ... ?" and I answer, "Phyllis ... that is ... well ... bats." Halloween spectres—vampirenesses—hover over reality. (Well we know fiction is far more real than the real.) "To judge all bats by the vampire is the same way people used to shoot every hawk they saw because one hawk stole the chicken," said a *Wall Street Journal* article of quite a few years ago. The same article points out that "riding on the shovels and trowels of the organic craze and a boom in home gardening, guano is undergoing a stunning revival ... entrepreneurs ... are battling over a big share of the thriving market." Another article from the same publication concentrates on the avid use of bat guano as fertilizer for the growing of marijuana.

Bat guano apparently does wonders for any growing thing—black peppercorns, tomatoes, whatever—and in the Far East it has long been known that bats signify good luck, happiness, fertility, and perchance long life. Aesop expressed antipathies for bats, calling them prevaricators (such a wonderful euphemism for liars). Could it be trepidation of the dark, their silent communications, that knocks bats into the realm of the fearful?

Red fox at the edge of the reedgrass could not care less about invisible sound waves bouncing off him. Last April, at our Passover seder we watched, red fox as still as the creek-side rocks, the waving reedgrass and moving water of the creek, a watercolor painting awash around him. He will wander to the garbage-burning plant down the creek if the pickings across from us prove poor. We sit watching, the door open for Elijah.

We cannot move. We are stilled in time. Less than fifty feet separate us from a feral foreign world. We hardly see him slink into the spicebush shrubs, but we do see him emerge, a large water rat grasped between his teeth, the rat's tail brushing the sand as red fox disappears into the shadows under the tulip tree.

I love such natural distractions at our annual seder, diversions I do not have to create for the disappearance of Elijah's cup of wine. For it must disappear. Why waste a glass of fine wine . . . ?

12

"... sound has a necessary connection with the world's unquiet, with its looseness and free play—its processes and vitality—and with our looseness in it. Something thuds into a listener's awareness on hearing a mattock bite into a root. Other sounds slide over awareness or rub along it, or scratch or saw into it. ...

"... We are to a degree continuous across the intervening air with what moves with us in one commonality of vibration, because the sounding of air has been galvanized by the source of sound into acting as a vibrant connective tissue."

DAVID BURROWS,

Sound, Speech, and Music, 1990

 It was a constant of my childhood, and beyond, to my young womanhood, until his early death—my father's left hand firm upon my shoulder, his right hand pressing his stethoscope against my child-chest, my ribs, my back, often pulling the instrument from his ears, pressing an ear against me. "Breathe deep ... mouth open ... try to cough ... again." Then he would talk to me. "Ausculation of the chest," he would say, "Listening to the rattling and rales of your lungs for medical diagnosis tells me if you are better than yesterday, or worse."

I would know when he began his longer discussions how ill I was, that asthma or pneumonia had again caused congestion inside my thoracic cavity, that he was filling the air with interesting words to grasp my attention, testing the degree of my alertness, my illness. Listening to the percussive patter inside my body, tapping my back sharply with his finger, he would say, told him much about my heart and lungs. Resonance reverberating back to him from those air- or water-filled places gave him information to evaluate, data from which he elicited the current state of my fragile health. Grandiloquent phrases, irresistible new words, odd facts and history meant I was still quite ill. He left them with me, weightless, invisible in the air of my bedroom. They would sink slowly like dust into my dictionary and a 1942 set of the *Encyclopedia Britannica* at my bedside where I would later search for them. Early I knew that when the head of wild red hair lifted its ear away from me, was silent, I was getting well, would soon have to return to school.

Watching my father, I always assumed a doctor listens, and to more than erumpent rasps received by stethoscope or ear. In the office of my current physician, on the window-ledge beside his desk, there is a small framed drawing of a stocky bemused-looking man (quite resembling my physician). He is at utter ease, leaning back in a chair. A penciled-in cartoon cloud floats over his head with the words "Are you listening?" "When I let my patients talk," he tells me, "I learn more about them, their needs, what I can do for them, than any crisp listing of medical history ... so I listen." Long before I began asking my geneticist sister about ultrasonography I was aware of medical acoustical sensing, a physician's awareness of body sounds and their meanings.

My father would talk to me between taps on my back. His attention to his tappings on me, he once said, was not original to him or to fellow physicians he frequently asked to look me over, but were accredited to another Austrian born near him (some two hundred years earlier), a physician fascinated by diseases of the lungs and thorax. Leopold Auenbrugger, in the mid 1700s, noted old ways of determining degrees of wine and beer fermentation. Traditionally the level of gas within kegs was estimated by knocking on the sides of kegs, listening to the resulting sound, appraisals grasped this way quite accurate to a long-time brewer. Perchance, Auenbrugger thought, this percussion method could be applied to medical practice. Still, it would be more than a century before a French physician would place a foot-long perforated wooden cylinder upon the chests of his patients, listening to the rumblings of their hearts and lungs, correlating the sounds he heard with diseases he found in autopsy studies. I first read about René-Théophile-Hyacinthe Laënnec's invention, the stethoscope, when I was eleven, plunging through books at my bedside. Being ill was so much more interesting than being well and going to school.

Time is eclipsed. The brewers, Auenbrugger, Laënnec, my father become steps away from present medical uses of ultrasonic imaging, a modern percussive technique wherein a computer flashes an analytic map on a television-like screen, a reflection of acoustic pulses sent into the body by a probe touching the skin. My *Myotis* seeks the size, the shape, the features, the farness or nearness of prey by sending forth ultrasonic sound waves that will return to him vibrating, illustrations his ears know how to read. So, too, a tiny transducer, emitting sound waves on a high frequency level beyond human hearing, scans the surface of the skin, traveling through liquid inside the body, a natural transmitter of sound. Echoing images bounce back to the computer monitor, transformed in instants into a charcoal-like rendering of lines and shadings on a piece of paper, interpretive art ready to by studied by masters.

Unheard sound producing miracles, yet even within the parameters of the scientific sphere, requiring that uncertain quality, the skilled reader/listener.

A still-beautiful eighty-one-year-old woman, argumentive, so alert, nearly blind by the ravages of two optic genetic diseases, sits in a small room next to a machine that resembles a large word processor/computer. She sees light, dark, occasional letters with a magnifying glass always with her, "and don't forget colors!" she declares, decisive ineluctable evidence that her hearing is sharp, that some sight still exists, denying the reality that one hour earlier she could not identify a large *E* cast on a wall in a darkened room. "Yes, I see colors!" Vehement, needing as always that the last word be hers.

I am sitting opposite her in the small room watching her lips in active conversation with a cornea specialist. His back faces me. I cannot see what he is saying. I want to know. It cannot be helped. He knows I cannot hear him . . . but his concentration is on this carefully combed woman in a stunning silk print blouse sitting beside an ultrasound monitor. Her optimism, her bravado disclaim impending total blindness, belie a desperate fear I know floats barely beyond her words. Her sturdy heart, her relatively good physical condition give voice to a fierce arrogance that masks what she does not want to think about . . . independence is slipping away from her.

We have been in the ophthalmology department of this large hospital for hours. Several physicians, including a glaucoma specialist, a retinologist, this man about to peer behind her scarred cornea, have given her exquisite unhurried time. She closes her eyes. Listening with my eyes I know she is responding to a request from her doctor. He swabs a jelly-like substance over her left eyelid. There seems little hope for residual sight in her right eye, overcome by glaucoma and Fuchs dystrophy (a disease of the cornea that besets several people in our family). Our hopes are for a cornea transplant for her left eye, attacked only by Fuchs. How much sight exists behind the damaged cornea?

The physician presses messages on a keyboard, brings a probe close to Mother's closed eyelid. Grey-white pictures appear on the screen. Painless acoustical impulses, ultrasonic sound waves are weaving through the fluid of Mother's left eye, returning as graphic medical messages. It all takes seconds. More keys are pressed. A printout is quickly clipped, stapled to the growing file on Mother's eyes.

A miracle of sound stilled in time. In this tiny room with its high-tech late-twentieth-century equipment I feel suddenly akin to the 1877 world of Thomas Edison, a world listening to his curious invention, the phonograph. I am hushed by wonder at the sonogram of Mother's inner eye. What astonishment must have rippled through thinking when Edison first captured, conserved, re-created on tinfoil the fleeting evanescence of sound.

When my children were mere beginnings, tiny miracles inside me, I would talk to them. Dearest child, I would say, the geese are here from the north . . . it is nearly time for you. Or, Dearest child, listen, I am writing my thesis about fairy tales . . . let me read one to you. And I did, and since a discussion of horror in children's literature was the essence of my dissertation my little ones listened to well over one hundred versions of the more than three hundred extant variants of the Cinderella theme and, too, to endless dwarf tales—"Bluebeard" and the poetic, tranquil, suddenly chilling "The Juniper Tree"—all interspersed with Chopin études, Mozart sonatas, and always the mathematical non-chalance of Bach concerti and keyboard variations, an attenuation of mood after even the grimmest of Grimm. I wanted my children, once they got here, to allow themselves to be affected by alternate realms of feeling.

I never questioned their listening to me although I never addressed them by name, saying, Robert, listen! or, Laura, you are quiet, nearly ready for the family bassinet, or, Janice, I cannot wait to hug you. I never used their names, always murmuring "Dearest child," the way I still address all letters to them in the far places where they now lead their grown-up lives.

I could not say Robert, Laura, Janice. Perhaps they were Rachel, Louis, Jesse . . . alternate choices. Rachel and Lauren, Alex and Jenny, my recent grandnieces and grandnephew, knew no such uncertainty from their parents. Amniocentesis revealed halfway whom to expect.

Doctors listen to a nonalive voice, sounds they cannot hear produced by sophisticated diagnostic tools that convert ultrasonic echoes into visual reports. Instrumental listening. Ultrasound combined with colored images of blood flow can detect ovarian tumors in the very earliest stages. And obstetricians send high frequency sound waves through amniotic fluid to determine exact stages of pregnancy, to see if multiple births might occur, to check fetal growth, to screen for fetal defects. A tiny murmuring transducer we cannot hear scans the surface of a woman's abdomen, or might scan the uterus directly through the vagina. Tissues, portions of the beginning child receive, reflect particulars as minute as one or two millimeters. Shadings appear on a monitor differing by cell structure, translations of a language we can only know visually.

A sonogram reveals the fetus and its environment in intimate detail. A fetal eye, a minuscule mouth sometimes sucking a Lilliputian thumb. (*Nature* magazine recently reported a current study by three researchers at a university in Belfast, observations giving substantial evidence "of a behavioural asymmetry in the fetus—a preference for sucking the thumb of the right hand." Using ultrasound they could not contro- vert the findings, "a clear bias for sucking the thumb of the right hand, only 12 of 224 [women observed] (5.4 per cent) fetuses favouring the left.")

Ah . . . clues to such a personal aspect of us, our handed- ness, visible for inspection, scientific consideration, long before we become aware, if we are left-handed, that we are different. Does such significant early-determined laterality infer logical or creative approaches to living, the dominance of the left or right side of the brain? Many people in my prolific wide-ranging family are left-handed, many others ambidextrous (as am I). Some of us lead logical orderly lives, some creative rambling existences, still others zoom off in unfathomable unpredictable directions. How extrapolate the inferences of prenatal thumb-sucking preference, how theorize such intimations of future life paths to be taken? Will there someday be no surprises left for the becoming parent . . . ?

Oh yes. The most scientifically studied sonogram cannot alter, make ordinary the wonder of that first grey-toned shadowed showing, that early ultrasonic rendering of the forming person-to-be. "The first picture for the album," my geneticist sister calls it.

And yes. Still, with all hints of the known . . . an enigma, a mystery, a question. A baby.

It is hot, in the nineties, humid heavy air hanging over the creek. "Typical Long Island summer day," my daughter laughs. We are talking long-distance, she on a Caribbean island where she is studying veterinary medicine, her island so hot, so bug-ridden in this warm season that now her home-island in New York is almost appealing. She knows my energy is low on days like this. I tell her I am sipping vodka-and-tonic as part of my research.

I am an archaeologist digging for sound, for its origins, its wondrous manifestations both hidden and overt, its beginnings, its middles, its unhearable far reaches. I discover, searching in the realm of ultrasonic vibrating sound waves beyond the limits of human hearing, that one of the industrial uses of ultrasound is the foaming of beverages. Carbonated beverages are never as perfect, as zestful as after the initial pouring after opening, the reason I purchase tonic and seltzer in small bottles rather than economy-priced larger ones. "Air content," notes one of my husband's engineering reference works, "which determines the life of a carbonated beverage, is reduced by foaming the bottles or cans before capping." The ultrasonic power required is minimal. Hence that first sprightly headiness on sipping that just-uncapped pressurized carbon dioxide. Then air rushes into the uncapped bottle diluting not only the remaining drink but eventually the effect of the process that produced the enlivening vigor of that first imbibing. Gone the distilled refreshing from an ultrasonic zap (that drink is flat . . .).

I tell my distant little one that I can never drink vodka-and-tonic again without thinking about the Curies, appealing to her scientific sensibility, her questioning immediately there. Pierre and his brother Jacques established the beginnings for the study of ultrasonics and its uses by defining in 1880 the phenomenon of piezoelectricity, a discovery which made the future of ultrasonics accessible.

Piezoelectricity—its prefix taken from the Greek *piez* (*ein*), to press—is a method of producing electricity, or electric polarity, by pressure on a nonconducting crystal such as quartz, sugar, rochelle salt, calamine, topaz, tourmaline, boracit, sodium chloride, zinc sulfide. Pierre Curie, listening in his laboratory, observed an electrical response (a scientific listening, instrumentally observed)—a response that occurred when a crystal such as quartz was placed under pressure. He saw too that the reverse happened—that under an electrical pressure the crystal would compress or expand causing the crystal to vibrate, sound waves so rapid they were inaudible to the human ear. Curie had discovered a way of creating ultrasonic vibrations. Certain crystals were capable of sending sound and receiving sound, sonic and ultrasonic, most of it beyond the receiving ability of the human ear.

The transmitting of sound is dependent on the mere speck, mere granule vibrated, its finite quantity and quality, its essential architecture the causation for the forming and shape of an acoustic wave. Everything about the sound produced depends on the nature of the medium through which the sound passes, especially its elasticity.

The piezoelectric phenomenon had been known well before the brothers Curie began their experimentation. When certain crystals were heated scientists had noted the appearance of electrical charges; however research prior to the Curies' investigations had resulted in ambivalent interpretations of piezoelectricity and its potential uses. Applying rare geometrical insights to crystals, especially to quartz and tourmaline, Jacques and Pierre concluded that the substances underwent changes, expanding or contracting depending on the direction of the electrical field in which they were placed. Most important was the response, which was rapid, sometimes producing as much as a billion vibrations per second. Piezoelectric crystals could be used both as sources of sound waves and as receivers, sending out vibrating sound. Depending on the pressure implemented and the intimate personal components of the crystal, that sound could be from within the audible human range to vast spheres beyond our hearing, to high ultrasonic frequencies.

Oh! the listening out there!

Consider the electronic resonation that occurred shortly after London's Royal Festival Concert Hall was constructed in 1951. It was soon apparent that the reverberation time for lower frequencies (the time it took for such sounds to die out) was too short. Electronic resonators placed in the ceiling increased the reverberation time, providing the ebbing of tones more in keeping with a composer's or a performer's intent.

But in the 1880s Pierre and Jacques Curie's discovery was

deemed of little use beyond the solving of certain scientific contradictions, oddnesses noticed, until then unexplained. Piezoelectric industrial uses were visionary until World War I when a physicist student of Pierre Curie, Paul Langevin, thought of using piezoelectric quartz to locate enemy submarines, and to experiment with underwater soundings by using Curie's method to produce high frequency sound waves.

Curie had demonstrated how to reflect such waves, how it was easier, the shorter the length of the sound wave, thus producing ultrasonic vibrations that could be used, for instance, to penetrate thicknesses of water. Langevin, fiddling in his laboratory in 1915, discovered what he called sonar (an acronym for *sound navigation and ranging*), a system of echolocation *Myotis* could have told him about (were such communication possible . . .).

Paul Langevin, listening to exploding crystals in the inner sanctum of his laboratory, thought of sonar mainly as a way for ships to detect icebergs. By 1917 he had his technique worked out. It would not see effective use until after the First World War when the German ship *Meteor*, on an expedition using sonar, discovered the mid-Atlantic ridge in 1922, a noteworthy mark benefiting the science of oceanography, a finding, alas, that did not rouse excitement in the ship's promoters. The *Meteor* sailing forth fully equipped with sonar that could measure ocean depths had a mission, a grand enterprise that would be unsuccessful, one that did not purposefully include the study of underwater geography: the *Meteor* was designed with its new sonar detection systems to recover gold from the ocean floors, dumped there in ships the Germans had methodically sunk, gold the German government planned to use to repay war debts. In the European war crises of March–April 1940, the French navy would invite Paul Langevin to use his knowledge and research on ultrasonic depth finders. Find those German submarines.

Did Langevin surmise that sonar would utterly change, revolutionize the science of oceanography? That the floor of the ocean at unguessed-at depths would lose much mystery? That even I decades later could utilize a rather less sophisticated ultrasonic device—a fish-finder—to follow the furious flow of bluefish bursting in late spring through the creek barely brushing the surface and sometimes bursting above it in wild longings and leaps, yet the seen just the tip of a Langevin iceberg, the creek filled with fish at all levels below. And it would be nearly twenty years more before the use of such sound waves would be applied to the field of medicine. In the late 1950s Dr. Ian Donald would be the first physician to use ultrasound to examine an unborn child, somewhere in the wild hills of Scotland.

The utilization of piezoelectric crystals to produce sonic and ultrasonic sound waves is with us in uncountable ways. Take the stabilizing of oscillating frequencies of electromagnetic circuits for radio broadcasting stations. And an inventor/manufacturer I met at a dinner party last month told me that if it were not for ultrasound, modern warplanes could not be produced. To be able to machine the innumerable intricate varied odd shapes into large titanium parts, sophisticated equipment is needed. Only an ultrasound cutting tool can slice through metal with such precision. The cutting tool itself becomes excited by ultrasonic vibrations enabling precise cutting of the metal. The actual cutting is done by cavitation—the explosive collapse of bubbles—which cause destruction of material. An ultrasonically-guided cutting tool vibrates fluid running over and around metal, creates a bubble breakdown at the point of touch, a swift clean-cut edge. When your dental hygienist cleans your teeth with a drill-like contrivance shooting water all over your mouth she is using equipment guided by the same principle as creating airplanes. The actual cleaning is done by cavitation. You have seen cavitation happening when water comes to a boil and it is there while you are sipping champagne, watching the erupting effervescence.

Transmitting acoustic waves on any level of audibility is dependent on the vibration of particles within the medium through which the wave is traveling. The elasticity of the medium, its range of ability to expand and contract, defines how each particle in that medium will react, oscillate in its own mini-orbit, and return, resuming its original inert form as the sound wave progresses past it. My husband Harvey, wandering through an old power-producing plant proposed for renovation, uses piezoelectric units—ultrasonic transducers—that take electric energy and convert it to acoustic energy, making it possible to check the thickness of old pipes, check for cracks in the metal otherwise undetectable. Sound waves unheard send aged particles vibrating, the results telling an engineer conditions of stress and weakness produced by age and use. Harvey listens to things I could not care less about . . . yet how wonderful to know these odd places where listening extends. I cannot imagine listening to an old buried pipe with interest, rising excitement. Harvey can. Listening is everywhere.

Ultrasonics—high-intensity sound waves—are applied in two ways, according to the direction of need or intent. Low-amplitude waves (lesser energy, lesser loudness sent forth) are used for material testing, locating structural problems, detecting structural cracks, faults, measuring thicknesses of materials, all usually invisible to an engineer's eye, all detected by a transducer generating electric impulses through a liquid to the test object. Flaws, separations are detected; porosity, lack of fusion with the structural differences of materials—plastics, glass, new or old concrete, rubber, ceramics—all taken into consideration by the known way ultrasonic reverberations respond to the particular medium. I listen to these wonders of discovery each evening as we dine al fresco, Harvey telling me the details of his day as night herons fighting for certain rock stances along the creek issue forth mind-grating squawks I cannot hear. Of Harvey's ultrasonic findings—the Curies would be so pleased. I tell him, too, the Curies could not be happier knowing the uses low-amplitude ultrasonic waves provide for medical diagnoses. (The uses for burglar alarms would not impassion them as much, I am sure . . . was there need for such wariness in 1880?)

High-amplitude ultrasonics (waves of greater energy and loudness) are used for cleaning processes, drilling, soldering, welding, with a multitude of biological and chemical applications, including some medical therapy and sonar. Cleaning? A bath ultrasonically agitated erodes dirt encrusted on immersed objects (applied surely only to machinery, not woman [or man], although my reference does not elucidate on this particular). Sonar detection of underwater objects is one of the older uses of ultrasonics, using the pulse-echo, Doppler effects (oh *Myotis* . . . you knew this all along).

Pierre Curie's studies led him on—as intense studies have a way of doing—to further-reaching realms in mathematics and physics. Could he ever have imagined, immersed in his laboratory (the place where he lived most of his personal and practical-livelihood worlds), the technological uses derived from his research that would dominate 1990s thinking? "Ultrasound," an article in *Forbes* (April 1990) said, "is the ultimate workstation . . . grown into a $700 million business." Or the study of exploding gas bubbles that consume the moments of scientists in a university in Illinois using "ultrasound, or sound pitched beyond human hearing, to create . . . turbulent micro-environments."

Pierre may have known his English contemporary, Sir Francis Galton, best known today not as the meteorologist he was (his 1863 publication still the basis for many current weather maps), or for his studies in heredity and his founding of the field of eugenics (that accepted many of the viewpoints of his cousin Charles Darwin), but as the inventor of the Galton whistle, probably the first instrument to use ultrasonic sound, creating high shrieks existing for the dog world, beyond human knowing, by a jet-blast of high-pressured air through a narrow slit of sharpened metal. Sir Francis's basic design, hardly altered, appears in modern renderings, silent signals to dogs wandering your backyard acreage, sheep-herding or on duty in security patrol systems, a sound piercing to a creature whose auditory system is open to it, a sound blissfully unheard by you and me. Galton's whistle is small, can be operated by your hand pressing an atomizer bulb inside your jacket pocket generating a high frequency sound. The simplicity of such a power source generates many kinds of whistles and sirens. In the early 1900s Julius Hartmann's designs implemented air (and gas) jets to generate acoustic waves. A modified use of the Hartmann generator uses an ultrasonic frequency to trigger the automatic opening of garage doors.

A few years ago (*New York Times*, September 10, 1990) I read that "more and more motorists are counting on whistles, mirrors, and other measures to help dodge a growing traffic menace: deer." Diversions and alarms of all sorts are being offered to the public—"truckers, highway safety officials, wildlife managers"—to minimize the dangers (everpresent from the soaring deer population) of wild deer dashing into the path of oncoming vehicles. Whistles seem the best although the state of Colorado has built underpasses under highways for deer to get to the other side of the road. Have the deer passed their getting-to-the-other-side-of-the-road-safely tests? They are used to the open, the wild. They are not used to being herded. So alternatives are in production for the motorist who does not want to slam into a deer, killing it and causing major destruction to his car or truck (and he may not even like the sudden supper, venison prepared in its many culinary possibilities). "More than twenty companies market small ultrasonic whistles that mount on car or truck bumpers and emit a shrill tone at high speeds. The whistles ... , inaudible to humans, are intended to startle deer and keep them off the road, but skeptics say they do not work."

One such device marketed by a New York State firm costs about twenty-five dollars, "relies on air rushing through a two-inch, bullet-shaped tube at speeds higher than thirty-miles-per-hour to emit a tone that the company says can be heard by a deer up to a quarter mile away." Collisions, claim the company, have become less frequent, prompting state police in Kansas, Iowa, and California to have as part of the equipment on their patrol cars these deer-scaring ultrasonic whistles.

It does not always work. "We found that you needed a straight shot for deer to hear them," said a spokesperson for the California Highway Patrol. A patrol car careening around a corner would suddenly lose its deer audience. And a number of the deer, even on the straight shot, were intelligent enough to hide behind trees. Listening is everywhere. Just look at the attempts that have been made to scare birds by using high frequency sound. True, city fathers, dead architects turning over in their graves, are appalled at the great damage done to the stonework of buildings by the droppings of flying creatures roosting or resting on such structures. And landing fields of airports must surely be kept cleared of birds just pausing there. Cockpit enclosures, props, and who knows what else can be smashed beyond repair by the impact of flying birds meeting head-on aircraft at the immense speeds now common. Consider the roosting seabirds that tend to rise in the path of seaplanes when such aircraft are zooming off or alighting. Sirens, ultrasonically powered, beam energy sound over a bird-infested area with horns that focus the high frequency sound. It bothers the birds more than a bit at first and some will fly off, but birds are resilient creatures and will eventually return, resuming their songful domain, accepting the sound interference, becoming accustomed to it, after a short while unworried by it, canceling out its irritation, ignoring it. How human.

What would Pierre and Jacques Curie and their colleague in their continuing physics research, Pierre's wife, Marja (Marie) Sklodowska, have thought of a *New York Times* advertisement describing the latest technology for ridding one's home or place of work of "mice, rats, roaches, bats, fleas, spiders and other pests [that] make life miserable." A machine (for a mere $69.95) delivers "a tremendous blast of ultrasound that is inaudible to humans and pets, but that sounds like an onrushing 747 to pests . . . so totally disrupts their nervous system that they'll leave your home within a few weeks—never to return . . . no poison, no mess." The pitch—the loudness—is adjustable to zap at larger annoyances such as raccoons, pigeons, rabbits, deer.

With the toll-free number, I sent for a more comprehensive description of this modern wonder that would create a "hostile environment" for pests. At certain settings the sounds are apparently audible to humans: " . . . it may be necessary to restrict use of this mode around people because the sounds may be annoying." The loud pitch intended to repel birds, deer, coyotes, raccoons, and other wild animals "should be restricted around people, or in residential urban environments." Individual paragraphs advise on repelling rodents, cockroaches, insects, spiders, bats, fleas, a variety of flying disturbances which find their way into your habitat with no open doors or windows, squiggling through window slits or screens, seeming deterrents. The pamphlet advises not to bother trying to rid your life of them for they will be, with the purchasable instrument, "physically exterminated or removed . . . they will die of dehydration in 1–2 days."

An intricately gorgeous spiderweb of sophisticated design links my houseboat workplace this moment with the dock, a web continually evolving (with flies, other tiny insects caught here and there) for the last two weeks, persisting through last night's heavy thunderstorm which downed trees. The skilled spinner appears in the mornings, lapping early dew, considering her day's work. What would an ultrasonic zap do to her delicate creative neural network?

Raccoon and his kin swim over evenings, a nuisance if we are careless enough to leave bags of garbage unheaved into the provided boatyard bins. Stun him with an electrified ray? Even if he was once the source of demise of my beloved Precious, a rather large retarded feline? He is the natural world.

And *Myotis*—rid evenings of his flutterings? Deprive field mice from nestling under the eaves of my houseboat's roof in early fall? And the cockroaches—they do not stay, the waterlife here not to their liking (or is it the presence of too many mice and cats?).

In the *New York Times* ad for this ultrasonic repellent you are offered two for the amazing price of $139.90 (exactly double the price of one). And a third is free, with the compliments of the manufacturer.

To my little one's current island I mail boxes of bug repellent—squiffings to send anthropods, arachnids, myriapods, centipedes, millipedes just a distance from her, to make her utterly undesirable for pecking. Nothing lethal, the repellents, when they work, keep mini-winged creatures at a distance from my mini-sized child, do not stun brief life to utter numbness, do not vanquish essence, so brief an insect's earthly existence anyway. "Send tons of it," she ordered, first arriving there in the bug season. I remembered her careful diligent removal of earmites from my six cats, before she left, placing some near her microscope for late-night inspection. I know how she would feel about my arachnid weaver on her burgeoning web. I know she will understand, when I tell her, how carefully I readjust lines on this craft while the creation is there. Last year, in a lonely moment she placed a personals ad in her local western newspaper, answering the six responses with, " . . . I honk for cows . . . "

dered, drowned, kidnapped, hijacked . . . whatever. When the weather report comes on you do not hear it. You have tuned out listening.

But . . . not the hearing impaired person wearing hearing aids. We know it all, the calm, the clamor. We are x-spurts. Many of the subtle vibrations of the air, known as sound, do escape us. Some of those sounds that reach us we are unable to identify. We may hear soft faraway murmurs, shadows of the pitch and intensity of a sound we once knew. Or often sounds reach us transformed, such as the conversation I had this morning with a neighbor, nine-year-old Jodi, who wears two hearing aids, as I do. "Your cat sneezed," he said, staring into the cockpit of my floating home. "Which one?" I asked, glancing at my several lounging felines. Jodi looked at me with big eyes. "Does it really work?" At that point it occurred to me we were not having a real "conversation," an exchange of thoughts.

Jodi's mother nearby was laughing. She is used to us and our errors. She is an honorary x-spurt. What really transpired was: "Your cat has fleas." Jodi heard my response as "Wish one" and thought it meant that one should make a wish when you see a flea, so he asked, "Does it really work?"

Yes, we really are x-spurts on the meaning of language. We grasp meanings the average hearing person does not dream of. Our specialty, however, is background noise. For us, when our hearing aids are switched to "on," it is always there, difficult to tune out.

I hesitate to say aloud anymore, "It is awfully noisy here . . . " or something to that effect. The immediate response is, "You can hear it!" That must mean my hearing impairment is gone, cured, disappeared. After all, hearing impairment means you cannot hear. It is useless, but I explain anyway that my hearing aids do not replace sound. They amplify it ... *all* sound. Because they are simply mechanical, because my hearing aids cannot think, they cannot cancel out magnified background noise. They cannot discriminate, tune in to just what they wish to hear, as can the unimpaired human ear, with its perfect connection to the brain. Our ears, though a very old model, basically the same design our ancestors wore millions of years ago (except less hairy), have held up as functional for earth living remarkably well. That may be about to change.

Current environmental conditions and lifestyles have altered radically, especially in the latter half of this century. In the primeval forest the worst noise was probably the falling of a tree, or the thud of a brontosaurus as he succumbed to an enemy. In medieval Europe the loudest noise was probably the clink of a chain when a reader shifted the position of a library book that was chained to the wall. Even eighty years ago we did not have rock music, jet planes, radios, television, loudspeakers, subways, chainsaws, or an incredible machine I watched at work yesterday, called The Hammer. A road was being torn up. The Hammer, when in operation, would raise a device on its nose which was indeed a giant hammer. At each plunge of the hammer to the cement the truck jerked, vibrated, lifting wheels off the ground. Its driver was bounced off the driver's seat, then dropped down and immediately bounced up again. His mouth hung open, his eyes crossed, his head waggled from side to side. I watched, fascinated. "You all right, Joe?" someone shouted over the terrible noise. "Y-y-y-e-e-a-h-h-h . . . " After a few minutes Joe was lowered out of the cab. He could not stand up. It was someone else's turn, in the name of progress and efficiency, to enjoy this modern wonder. I noticed the drivers wore no protective ear plugs, helmets, nothing to reduce the destructive impact of their work experience.

I sit in a restaurant and it is noisy. I cannot, like anyone else with good hearing, listen just to the person I am talking to. I try. There is a blur of sound. I go to New York City and I am assaulted by pandemonium pounding on my head from every direction. I can turn off my hearing aids, unless I want to attempt a conversation with my companion. Often I resort to becoming the silent type. At a gathering of friends I must lure someone out of the living room for real talk. ("Let's walk in the garden . . . "—a comment sure to elicit odd glances if it is winter . . .)

It is astonishing that with all now known about the deteriorating effects of noise on the delicate instrument that is the human ear, we are still bombarded with man-made cacophony. Prolonged exposure to rock concerts, the subway, factory machinery, jet engines, all things we consider necessary to our daily existence, without taking measures to protect our ears, will eventually lead to permanent sensorineural hearing loss. It is estimated that a huge percentage of people in this country under the age of thirty have already suffered serious loss in the range of their hearing, something that would only have happened to most of them, if at all, at a much later age.

When is sound noise? When is the presence of sound too much for the healthy maintenance of one our great evolutionary gifts—hearing?

We measure sound by a unit called a decibel. The decibel system begins at 0, the faintest sound the human ear is capable of hearing. A decibel level of 10 means more than a ten-times increase in the intensity of the sound because the perceived loudness of sound doubles every 10 decibels. The blast of a jet engine at take-off is 150 decibels, or 1,000,000,000,000,000 times as intense as the faintest whisper we can hear.

Ordinary conversation is generally at about 65 decibels. Sounds become uncomfortable to most people at around 100 decibels. Above 120 decibels we feel an annoying sensation in the ear. Still more intense sound causes not only pain but sometimes temporary or permanent hearing loss. Hearing impairment is common after exposure to certain kinds of noise—gunfire explosion, operators of boilers and stamp-presses, riveters, people who work around jet engines.

In future generations, perhaps all humans will be x-spurts at an early age. Or perhaps technology will apply itself to find a way to put silencers, quietening devices, on some of the more noisy aspects of our lives.

And perhaps someone soon will invent a more perfect hearing aid, one that will amplify, just to the right tone, just what we want to hear. (Leonardo, where are you today?)

Meantime, imperfect as they are, we x-spurts are as happy

that hearing aids exist as were people when the first autos and airplanes appeared. Though not yet perfect, hearing aids add a significant dimension to an x-spurt's life. Unfortunately, hearing impaired x-spurts are about to lose their prestige, their uniqueness. As the decibel level of daily life escalates, x-spurts will be everywhere. Arrays of creative inventiveness will appear in the form of designer hearing aids, perhaps in colors, or bejeweled, labeled perchance by Dior, Chanel, Gloria Vanderbilt. Competition will be keen. Like jeans, jogging shoes and jazzy T-shirts, nearly everyone will have them.

In the Antarctica winter of 1933 Admiral Richard Byrd, manning a weather observation post single-handedly, wrote in his journal: "Took my daily walk at 4 P.M. . . . I paused to listen to the silence. . . . The day was dying, the night being born—but with great peace. Here were imponderable processes and forces of the cosmos, harmonious and soundless. Harmony, that was it! That was what came out of the silence—a gentle rhythm, the strain of a perfect chord, the music of the spheres, perhaps."

Is an Antarctic late afternoon as mute now in the 1990s, stilled by all but the natural, "sonic" sound intrinsic to untouched far reaches, feral pristine unpeopled places . . . or is Byrd's "gentle rhythm" subverted, his ice-cap harmony distilled at 4 P.M. by the raucous engines of a cruise ship churning into the chill ocean dark, casting off from a tourist stopover. The "imponderable processes and forces of the cosmos" thunder quiescent messages at every hour, everywhere on earth. Surely I could not hear them even with perfect hearing. To "hear" Admiral Byrd's great quiet, feel his gentle rhythmic music one must find pockets of hush, soft near-soundless silence. Where to seek it—does it exist—utter pockets of silence in modern life?

Noise is omnipresent. A *New York Times* article (aptly titled "Research on Noise Disappears in the Din") quotes an environmentalist who suggests that "the trouble with noise is that it's not visible like garbage, oil spills and other pollutants." It is hardly news anymore to read that noise in excess of acceptable levels to the ear can cause moderate to severe hearing impairment—but I was startled to read (immediately turning off my hearing aids) the physiological and psychological impact of noise met on any ordinary day at home, on the job, in recreational activities. Links have been ascertained between exposure to noise and high blood pressure, fatigue from effort to plod through urban din, and in California researchers have recorded "a higher rate of cardiovascular deaths, strokes, suicides and murder among 200,000 residents of a flight-path corridor near Los Angeles International Airport." It is anticlimactic to read that "experiments show that noise modifies behavior" and that "the noise situation is simply awful."

And alas! The stymied research team in London, studying hearing damage and deafness in young adults, having a difficult time rounding up a control group of sixty subjects. Finding children who had not been exposed to loud and amplified music seemed, after great searching, impossible. The researcher in charge has not altogether despaired. He is looking for foreign exchange students whose exposure to amplified music has been minimal or nonexistent, and he has found students whose religious orientation objects to rock music.

At 4 A.M.—some nights—I talk to Admiral Byrd. It is 4 A.M., I say, a magical hour, no longer quite night nor yet day. I tell him I can see time happening, I can see the new day being born. I listen to the silence.

Silence surrounds me, touches the very air I am in. A small cluster of stars wings eastward overhead, the night lights on an airplane lifting out of the nearby airport, its engines the music of my modern-world sphere, ungentle rhythms I cannot hear. The black mass that is land across the creek is alive with creatures of night, in retreat to rare refuges close to rocks and dark jetties. Night herons fly into trees in the not-quite light while Venus hangs low in the sky. I write with ease, yellow pad in my lap, sharpened pencils nearby, in the stillness of A.M. hours. The chance of interruptions is small. It is unlikely the telephone will intrude, a reminder of the jangling day-world. Unexpected visitors who cannot understand that I am at work when I am at home will not appear.

There is a stillness, a cessation to all claims on me that lends to creating in the after-midnight hours. In my cockpit room the world of people is dormant. A ship's deck becomes my private Antarctica, though a short sail through the creek and the harbor brings the near New York City skyline into view, a reminder that I have not escaped the disturbance-edge of quiet, reached an utter pocket of silence. A marina in the Northeast is a beehive of activity half the year. The pursuit of leisure is frantic. It is not until the A.M. hours in summer—most hours in winter—that my Antarctica really comes here. There is a perceptible plunging of the fevered pitch after Labor Day. Real silence will not be heard until December. The ever-present aircraft from two large city airports will still be overhead, but motorcraft, sleek racing boats with huge engines and angry aggressive names (*Avenger, Outrageous, Revenge, Slammer, Blaster, The Scream*), idling through the creek toward Long Island Sound, their engines a pounding blast of 747-like power, will be gone. And too, the jet skiers. It is no wonder that one western anthropologist suggests that "one of the reasons Americans are so reluctant to carpool is that, for many, the commute is their Walden Pond—their only quiet time alone."

There are other Antarcticas. Muhammad, during the holy month of Ramadan, sought seclusion in the cave of Hera. Eighteen-year-old Tania Abei sailed around the world with only her cat for company. "On the open ocean, quiet was my environment. It became part of my being . . . I came to know every sound. Long before I could see it, I could feel the rumblings of an approaching ship." Reading that reminded me of Helen Keller in her ultimate silence. Alexander Graham Bell took her to Niagara Falls. Standing in a hotel lobby he placed her hand on a window pane so she could sense the precipitous pitching of the rushing river thundering over the precipice. Not unlike the way I wash dishes—barefoot at my galley sink, so I can feel the vibration of my craft's water pump, the only way I can tell if it is working correctly.

I think about a man in Seattle who calls himself The Sound Tracker. He regularly takes off to the wilds of the Pacific Northwest with twenty thousand dollars' worth of sound equipment searching for what he calls an endangered species—places that are noise-free, areas of natural quiet. A noise-free experience, he says, is "the aural equivalent of looking at the Milky Way once you've gotten away, totally, from the ambient light of the city." His wild places "ring with the sound of quiet," as does Tania Abei's ocean and my creek. Our quiet places are not soundless. *Noise* is absent, the percussive pulse, the tremulous torrent of accumulated mechanisms and masses of people that permeates much of modern life, noise that a recent *Time* magazine article said is generally acknowledged as annoying . . . yet accepted. The director of the National Institute on Deafness and Other Communication Disorders, Dr. James Snow, Jr., says, "There is so much noise we're exposed to that we tend to become complacent about it."

Admiral Byrd would find his Antarctica changed. The waters surrounding Antarctica are subjected to explosions as scientists pursue seismic studies of sedimentary layers beneath heavy depths of ice. Underwater dynamite explosions have affected the hearing of Wedell seals who live in

Antarctica's McMurdo Sound, a profoundly sad loss for the deep-diving Wedells who live at murky depths where no light penetrates. They communicate with each other by emitting whistling sounds, a communication lost when their inner ears are damaged, leaving them in darkness and deafness.

It is 4 A.M. on Glen Cove Creek. I am exhilarated by cosmic silence however thundering it really is up there. Simone Weil thought there was poetry in the noise of the man-made universe, writing a paean to urban cacophony (*Simone Weil: A Modern Pilgrimage* by Robert Coles; Addison-Wesley, 1987):

> All noises have their meanings, they are all rhythmic, they fuse into a kind of giant respiration of the working collectivity... there are ... the metallic noises, the turning wheels, the bite of metal upon metal; noises that speak neither of nature nor of life, but of the serious, steady, uninterrupted acting of men upon things. Though lost in the great hum, one also dominates it ... through the wan hours of winter mornings and evenings when only the electric lights are shining, all the senses are participants in a universe where nothing recalls nature, where nothing is gratuitous, where everything is sheer impact, the painful yet conquering impact of man upon matter.

Someone listening to a rock concert, or a runner with earphones knowing only some uncosmic blare, share a love of a bursting sound they would not call noise. I watch a shooting star in the dying night silently dropping off the edge of the still-dark western sky. If there is noise to its violent rush through my universe I do not know it.

Writing in the night as I often do, rocked by keening winds I cannot hear, reminds me I am following in fine literary footsteps. George Sand, writing her novels in her nineteenth-century villa, would often take up her pen after an ardent night of lovemaking, while her lover, Frederic Chopin, slept.

Noise—sound that is uncomfortable—becomes such a personal assessment. I picture George Sand—quill, inkpot, parchment on a leather-inlaid mahogany desk—listening to the ineluctable snoring of her sleeping lover. Music, not noise, to her.

There are unexpected blessings to being deaf . . .

I am flat on my belly on the dock with a flashlight peering into three feet of low tide murky water, watching *Lophius americanus*, a study in ugliness. The wood of the dock conducts vibrations telling me lumbering steps are approaching. "Today . . . yes definitely today . . . I am going to kill that fucking bastard!"

I remind Donald, a neighboring houseboat liveaboard, that *Lophius* is not the cause of his nightly distress. He is confusing her with another supremely grotesque marine creature very noisy in its lovemaking that is keeping him awake nights. *Lophius*, a goosefish, horrifically repulsive in a scaleless slippery-skinned slimy body that is mostly huge head and three rows of menacing teeth, lies in the mud near our homes every summer, voraciously dining on cormorants, ducks, gulls, lobster, an occasional goose, hermit crabs, squid, an assortment of invertebrates, all gathered into a capacious mouth, jaw and lips fringed with fleshy flaps. The goosefish's appetite is notorious. Her sex life is violent, but silent. (Her mate attaches himself to her, his lips and tongue growing into her skin as the rest of him degenerates, except for his reproductive organs which continue to be active as he mates with her.)

Donald is not convinced. He knows the noise keeping many of the marina residents awake nights is caused by a supremely ugly fish. Could anything be as unprepossessing as *Lophius*? We have not seen *Opsanus tau*, an oyster toadfish whose amorous courtship grunts and growls punctuated by whistles and squeals emerging from his flexible vibrating swim bladder indicate loudly to the world that the time for making babies is at hand (i.e. at gill or flipper). Photographs tell me he is a viable contestant, along with *Lophius*, in any Ugliest-Undersea-Dweller contest that might someday be held.

Opsanus has remained elusive. The pseudo-ichthyologists among us on the dock have been stalking the tidal rock-strewn places for *Opsanus*, the Atlantic Coast cousin of *Porichthys notatus* whose muddy sea-bottom territory is the Pacific Coast. We know *Opsanus* is here, has sluggishly made his way toward shore with lusty urgings impelling his steady slow progress. His nightly stentorian romantic advances have announced his arrival. He has been present, if unseen, for weeks, since early June. We know he searches for a suitable nesting area near the jetties and shoal-water rocks before beginning his mournful bassoon-like crooning to attract mates to his chosen intertidal nesting site. His hum can have a frequency ranging from 98 to 108 hertz, on the discomfort side of listening.

Toadfish are a bottom-dwelling species, spending most of the year far offshore. From June through September they are lured to shallow waters by sexual longings to mate. Males are exemplary fathers, guarding the fertilized eggs until hatched (keeping the population explosion in control by eating the babes not quick enough to escape when born). The males are also an uncontrolled source of noise pollution through the summer months. The sonorous grunts, growls, irritating hums—variously described as something like an electric foghorn, or a helicopter in your room over your head, or a flight of B-17s flying low en route to a mission—are the impassioned iterations of a male toadfish sensing a companionable response.

In some perfectly lovely estuaries and bays—where the sandy/rocky conditions are just right—the nights from June through September may be filled with more than the wing-beats of bats and the symphonic renderings of crickets: these are the likely breeding sites for toadfish young, and since *Opsanus* and *Porichthys* only sing their amorous songs when they expect reciprocation, the volume of sound depends on how many toadfish have found your gunkhole.

I had been blissfully unaware of these disturbances in the night, vying in volume level with stereos and generator pumps. This morning all three hundred pounds of Donald appeared, seeming more massive than usual, armed with a boathook. "If

Opsanus's courtship cavortings and moanings are getting to you," I suggest, ". . . bring Betty down below—save the top deck for October and thereafter when *Opsanus* leaves for the lower depths, until next June." We share, he and I, I remind him, acoustically insulated craft, his of steel, mine of wood. The melodic endearments of the toadfish penetrate fiberglass and ferro-cement hulls with ease. Wood and steel are apparently immune. You will not hear him inside.

The sun is rising, a brilliant oversized orange globe, lifting, as we watch it, into a hazy lifeless sky. Not a breath of wind stirs the reedgrass. Another typical hot, humid, Long Island July summer day. "By God!" Donald says, almost smiling. "That screwing Romeo has stopped! Maybe he's dead." I had noticed no difference in the morning air. It still held the soft stillness of dawn. I tell Donald, no, our toadfish is resting after a night of vigorous social obligations. Sit down, I invite. I'll tell you a sexy story.

There are old-time liveaboards in the Richardson Bay area of California, at the northern end of San Francisco Bay, who say they have heard the annual reverberating hum for as long as they can remember. Just part of the summer noise level from June through September. It ends abruptly in October. It is not a sound too discernible in the open air, rather seems to resonate through the hulls of the nearly 500 houseboats of the Sausalito residents that reside afloat. That is, through some of them.

The floating residents of the small town of Sausalito once consisted largely of fishermen and artists who accepted the hum, if they heard it at all, as they accepted all the natural phenomena of their chosen habitat. Most of them never noticed it, living, as they did, on discarded rusting steel barges and floating homes erected upon World War II landing craft, heavily built wooden structures sold, after the war, as surplus. (My houseboat, the good ship *Bette Anne*, is one of these. Not hearing the hum may have nothing to do with my deafness.)

The resonant tones of the love-starved toadfish seem to quaver and throb easily through modern man-made materials, hulls built of fiber-reinforced resins and ferro-cement, the foundation structures of the floating condominium-like homes that now abound in yuppy-overrun waters around Sausalito. The intensity of the deep drone arises from the mud shortly after sundown, an eerie din of rising decibels in the salons and staterooms as the impassioned loathsome lover drags the unprotesting object of his amatory arias beneath some chosen rocks to which she will attach about 200 eggs.

The newer liveaboards complained. It must be the local sewage treatment plant; it must be the Army Corps of Engineers conducting a military experiment; it must be the presence of extraterrestrials (Sausalito would be a delightful place to pause while traveling through the universe). Many were certain it was some inconsiderate person running a pump or generator at night (the floating craft are moored quite close, engendering an intimacy sometimes undesired). In the mid-

1980s complaints poured into the office of the Marin County Noise Advisor. One houseboater volunteered his services as an acoustical engineer, spending the greater part of summer nights out in the bay with divers and hydrophones. The besieged sewer pumps were eliminated as a possible cause, and then just as the researchers appeared temporarily stymied, the hum ceased. Of course. It was October.

Summer came again. It always does. The love songs, heard only as aggravating noise to those that heard it, commenced in June. The engineer and his associates felt that "finding the noise source would provide good exposure for business. Since we're all experienced acoustical and vibration specialists, we simply assumed this would be an easy problem to solve." They were, noted a magazine article about their endeavors, "damned if they'd let another summer pass without nailing the noise polluter."

Driving home from San Francisco State University, where he is a teacher of marine ecology, Thomas Niesen heard a news item on his radio. He laughed as he recalled studies he had made several years before in Monterey Bay. He called the acoustical engineer. "There was no doubt," he said, "that this was the sound of the plainfin midshipman (*Porichthys notatus*), also known as the singing toadfish."

The acoustical firm was stunned. A fish? They called a local aquarium director, a noted ichthyologist who was amazed no one had considered a biological cause. Had no one heard of *Porichthys*? "What," he asked, "makes noise at night and only in the summer? What's looking for romance at night and in the summer? Not machinery."

Toadfish were brought in for scientific study, but even after playing recordings of their singing to entice responses, they remained mute. At last a fisherman brought in a specimen in the midst of an ardent song, caught in a trap with other fish. Surely, proof.

There are still nonbelievers. Scientists are telling the houseboaters that fish do make noise. Pliny and Aristotle have both discussed this in their writings on natural animal occurrences. The Office of Naval Research, studying submarine sounds, discovered that the ocean depths are far from silent places. Significant levels of noise come from the echolocation of whales and porpoises; shrimp pop and snap; the creaks and croaks and yelps and groans and hoots of all sizes of fish permeate the underwater world. Ichthyologists know that fish noises are ordinary. Still, those unfamiliar with life beneath the surface of the sea are incredulous, even when the sources of sea noise are described. Just the underwater movement of a large marine creature—a whale, a shark, a grouper—causes a thumping, frequently loud, by the sudden displacement of water. Then there is the stridulent teeth-grinding screech created by a fish biting into the bony parts of prey. And fish produce sound by the flexing of muscles in a resonating chamber found in many fish called by several names—an air bladder, a gas bladder, a swim bladder, all of which act as a ballast chamber. A fish can effortlessly retain equilibrium at any depth it chooses by adjusting the density of this bladder to that of the surrounding sea. With their flexible bladder the Atlantic and Pacific toadfish produce a repertoire that does not make the human

Hit Parade, but surely promotes the prolific propagation of the species.

Skeptics intent on pursuing their own tunnel-vision view abound, and not only in Sausalito. One man "vows to nail the sewage plant . . . this fish stuff is just a big cover-up." The adventure of finding an erotic male in the midst of an enraptured tremolo was filmed and reported by Dan Rather on *CBS Evening News* (August 20, 1985). Rather's comment: "If you believe that, you believe frogs have hair." The next step, apprizing the public, was accomplished by circulating volumes of news releases and the selling of silk-screened T-shirts. Disbelief continued. The largest newspaper in Marin County stated:

> We don't believe for an instant that the drone keeping Sausalito houseboaters awake at night is caused by a bunch of romantic toadfish humming their version of the Indian Love Song . . . Only the species that developed the atomic clock, the digital watch, and the on-time European train is capable of creating such a commotion . . . The only animal capable of filling an entire bay with obnoxious sound is man.

The aquarium director mentioned earlier, commenting on the above, stated: "Such anthropomorphic arrogance could come only from someone unfamiliar with the screeching whine of a thumb-sized cicada, the bellow of a bullfrog, or the cacophony of crickets." He intimates the yuppification of the floating life can be seen in the urban attitudes they flaunt. "Modern Sausalitans are so urbanized they're all but ignorant of the springtime chorus of amorous animals . . .

the noises of nature have been drowned out by the machines of man."

The last step in solving this noise pollution problem—getting rid of it—remains undone. A few sporting humans tried to interrupt *Porichthys* in the dark of one summer night by dropping M-80 firecrackers. A few shock waves rippled across the bay, some flashing light. The toadfish remained unperturbed in their annual pursuit of brief ecstasy. They continued to hum.

"They are supposed to be quite tasty," I say to Donald, both of us watching our goosefish inhale a couple of dozen spring snappers each several inches long. "I could bake her whole with garlic ... you could use the head for some of your wonderful chowder ... in Europe I understand goosefish is a popular delicacy."

Neither of us reaches for our fishing nets.

14

"Listening is the application of the mind *to sounds which the ear . . . may or may not hear."*

PERCY C. BUCK,

1944

 I am in the best possible place in the world I could be at this pain-ridden moment (the world for this weekend being Worcester, Massachusetts, where I am visiting family). I am in the University of Massachusetts Hospital Emergency Trauma Center, early on a Sunday morning, after a terrible night of not knowing where to put my head. I am getting superb care.

Medically, that is. Does it matter, I keep thinking, now that I am about to get some relief from this torment, that after a few carefully directed sentences to me, the rest of the conversation, including instructions for care until I can get home to New York and my own otolaryngologist, are spoken behind my head where I cannot see the uttered words, a conversation with my husband that ignores me entirely? I am not unconscious (though I wish I was). I am only more deafened than usual, unable to wear my hearing aids. The physicians have been told I am a remarkable lip-reader. They comment on this initially. And then I am forgotten.

Something happens when I tell someone I am severely hearing impaired—when I say, please look at me directly so that I can see what you are saying. Something happens and I know what it is, a canceling out of the words I have said simply because I have *said* them. I have spoken in a clear voice, my speech understandable. My ability to speak well masks an unalterable fact—delivery of articulate speech does not mean that receiving another's spoken thoughts takes place. To comprehend conversation, I need to be stared at.

Ear infections are hardly new to me. No matter how careful I am about cleaning my earmolds, bacteria seem to find my ears a wonderful place to breed, thriving undisturbed while I wear my two hearing aids from the minute I arise until bedtime. Usually I am lucky, the bacteria choosing one ear at a time. While one ear is languishing, the other is functioning, not cutting me off entirely from the little hearing aid–aided hearing that I have (of course I much prefer to be a binaural woman). This Sunday morning is not one of the better ones. Both ears are being attacked at once.

This particular siege began several days before. I could not reach my favorite ear specialist. A second choice was equally unavailable. Ah, summer! I let a third unknown-but-highly-recommended earnest person peer into my mysterious canals. So I had not ignored the situation when I left for New England the next day.

I am sitting on a white-sheeted bed/table in a window-less-room thinking of the helicopter outside next to the car that has driven me here. I am here because after hours of trying to find an ear specialist who would see me at the crack of dawn on a Sunday summer morning, my mother-in-law had finally suggested a hospital emergency room.

This city has many excellent hospitals, yet I refused some very fine suggestions based on previous unforgettable emergency room experience. Not only my ears were hurting. I could not touch behind my ears or my jawbone or any part of my face without pain. I did not want anyone who did not know a lot about ears to touch me.

Midnight, the night before. I am sitting at the kitchen table, my head cradled atop my arms, moaning. True, I have a very low threshold of pain and have been known to complain loudly about a hangnail. Nevertheless, my suffering is believed and my husband's mother, trying to help me, is making telephone calls to physicians who cannot be reached on the weekend, or who will not see or respond to patients who are not their own. Hours before, the last moment before I had to remove my second hearing aid, I had spoken to my sister who had just driven her desperately ill husband hundreds of miles across a western desert to a university hospital. They were on vacation. "I had to get him to a teaching hospital," she said, "a place that would know how to care for a cancer patient . . . a place that would be sure to have specialists on call, or there."

During the night I recalled her words: "I need a teaching hospital," I said. The University of Massachusetts Hospital is only minutes from where I am staying. No one had thought of it. (A hug and special kiss for my sister!)

I am in a facility prepared for far more than my aching ears. A first doctor has called in a second, both talking briefly to me, more to my husband, showing me the "toys" they have spent some time searching for, instruments small enough to investigate my tiny convoluted canals, like a child's (in some ways I have never grown up). Drops of a topical anesthetic trickle into one ear. Magic! Instant no pain! I can see conversation happening around me even as they signal to me to flip over to investigate my other ear. I glance upward and backward at the two physicians and my husband, all involved in lively conversation, laughing. They leave, my two miracle workers, without even a last glance or word to me. "What was that all about?" I ask.

"Just instruction . . . " My husband is smiling, his wonderful dashing curled mustache a lip-reading challenge I have learned to navigate. I stand up, ready to leave, as the first doctor reappears, handing me prescriptions but speaking entirely to my husband. I am pain-free for the first time in days yet nettled with a different pain, the same cutting distress that occurs when I ask someone to repeat what has just been said, something I have not quite understood. "Oh . . . nothing" is the common response.

Nothing is nothing. To a hearing impaired person trying to grasp at everything, nothing is small, not a word is minutiae, so important is it to sense the essence of the ordinary happening around us. What stops us often is not our own verbal efforts to "hear" from the seen verbal and visual cues around us. It is the answers to asking that toss us off, reminding us we are relegated all to frequently to a place reserved for the mindless.

Is a mind that is alive unabled, something to be bypassed, ignored, if a sense is dysfunctioning? Would it have been so beyond imaginable medical procedure to have discussed the "what-to-dos" of my case facing me, allowing me to participate, to touch my husband's hand in the known way we have when I do not understand something, my touch on his hand the light hint that tells him I need amplification?

Would it have been so terrible, so beyond professional practice, to have included me in the details that concerned myself . . . ?

I tell this to my dear husband in the car driving back to our waiting family: even he who does more than anyone to describe the world of sound to me, even he, at times, isolates me.

"Yes," he muses, twirling his mustache, "I see . . . we excluded you . . . and at such a terrible moment . . . "

Besides instructions for my care, they were talking about sled dogs, a subject that arose as odd things do in casual talk because of previous comment about my hearing guide dog, Sheena. Irrelevant, perhaps, but really not. At any time I like to choose what to give ear—or eye—to. Why fail to assume, not even consider, that I might want to listen, in my own interpretive way, to something as interesting as commentary about sled dogs?

15

"Concentrate your will. Hear not with your ears but with your mind; not with your mind but with your spirit. Let your hearing stop with the ears, and let your mind stop with its images. Let your spirit, however, be like a blank, passively responsive to externals. In such open receptivity only can Tao abide. And that open receptivity is the fasting of the heart."

LAO-TZU,
604(?)–531 B.C.

 It is June, the sweet scent of moist earth and flowering trees across the creek floating through every opened porthole and hatch. The sun is rising over the southwest horizon, a swift spreading of salmon pink behind the incinerator stack. I am gathering breakfast dishes into the galley sink, turn at the touch of soft fingers on my shoulder. Harvey motions that I follow him, a naked creature, my Adam in our private Eden. The overhead hatch in the head lets in a rush of moist fertilized earth from the flower boxes on deck. Harvey points to a curved oak molding near the hatch. He had been about to turn on the shower when he saw her—for surely it is a her—ample, rounded, silent (males are smaller, near-gaunt, songful), "an insect of imposing appearance," J. Henri

Fabre so aptly described her, "with gossamer wings, broad and green, trailing long veils of finest lawn . . . a mask for Satanic habits." Feeding almost exclusively on live prey, the female *Mantis religiosa* "is the tigress of the peaceable entomological tribes, the ogress in ambush who levies a tribute of fresh meat."

Abstracted by her unexpected stately presence in our home, Harvey gave no thought to the possible danger of handling a mantis, a creature known for the raptorial power of her forelegs. He lifted her gently, placing her on deck just outside the overhead hatch. In seconds she returned inside, on the same curved molding. Harvey reached again for our visitor, carrying her quickly up our companionway steps to deck, to one of my thriving flower boxes. Oh no! Mantids, though predaceous, carnivorously on the alert for their next live snack, often settle rapaciously on greenery.

My mantis is nearly invisible in the leaves of my Mexican heather plant, sniffing intently at the delicate miniature rose-colored blossoms that I have nurtured, kept blooming inside by a sunny window all winter. Soon she veers from the vegetation, grasping in her pruning-hook-like forelegs a large spider, then a careless golden butterfly, defenseless victims as will soon be the males of her own kind, consumed head first, even as they mate with her.

In my nightgown I crawl close to the flower box. Will I be able to see her single ultrasonic ear nestled in a groove in her thorax near the underside of her abdomen, an ear tuned to the ultrasonic chirps of hungry flying bats, sounds inaudible to the human ear? Or do only male mantises have an ear?

A malevolent daring insect, a predator of power, the mantis, in the balance of life in the natural world, is also prey, a special morsel for a bat, expert at insect-snaring. An insectivorous bat's evening meal, a relishing of a variety of insects available at any moment, is a garnered feast gathered in the dark on the wing. If the bat's sonar detects a mantis in the air, it will be a male. The females of most mantis species do not fly.

Alas! a tasty male mantis as an hors d'oeuvre is an infrequent gastronomic treat for a bat. Too often a mantis outwits a bat, equipped as it is with a warning system, an ear that listens for the high frequency chirps of bats on their evening prowl. Within a tenth-of-a-second of detecting the nearing bat cries a mantis goes into a survival act, flipping and rolling in the air, spiraling in a spectacular power dive, an "evasive choreography" enabling the mantis to elude most bat advances.

My momentary mantis lingered briefly, digesting another spider and some fluttering morning moths. In earlier centuries we would have searched for her nest, roasting it in prescribed fashion, a twelfth-century remedy (ingested on an empty stomach) for belching, impotence, semen production, pain in the hip, asthma, gonorrhea and who knows what else. And we surely would have kept *her*, eventually grinding her thoroughly with a tropical croton bean, the combined medicinal value of the mixture so excellent for warts, convulsions, for the easy removal of arrows and knives embedded in wounds.

I would save—for close scrutiny—her remarkable ear.

A friend sent me a list of *Merker* words. Until now my knowledge of German has been limited to *Herr*, *Fräulein*, "Eine Kleine Nachtmusik," and my name, which my father said means "observer." Other *Merker* words leap out from odd places.

I stumbled on Baron Jakob Johann von Uexküll, a German biologist and comparative psychologist whose investigations into the sensory functioning of living beings led him to define the distinction between a live creature's *Umwelt* (environment) and its *Merkwelt* (perceptual world). Studying the auditory faculty of creatures, human and otherwise,

Merker—Old German: marker, scribe, score-keeper, fault-finder, critic. In Wagner's *Die Meistersinger*, the hypercritical guild secretary is addressed as "der Herr Merker."

bemerken—to observe, notice*

bemerkenswert—noteworthy, remarkable

merkwürdig—to be taken note of, peculiar, odd, strange

Anmerkung—note, footnote, reference

merken—to notice, realize, remember: "Pray you, mark me!"†

(*The Tempest*)

Merkmal—marker, monument, characteristic feature

Merkwürdigkeit—noteworthiness, oddity

Merkzeichen—mark, identifying characteristic

Merkbuch—notebook

Merkblatt—instruction sheet

---

* "*Ich habe es schon bemerkt.*"—"I have already noticed it."

† "*Merken Sie sich das!*"—"Be sure to remember that!"

von Uexküll asserted, in 1921, that almost no two species have the same sensory capacities. The *Merkwelt* of my cats, my dog, the wild red foxes, the numberless birds all sharing my immediate *Umwelt* have disparate visions of our mutual community life. A significant *Merkwürdigkeit* connects part of my *Merkwelt* with chance creatures of this creek: snails, starfish, flies, bees, are completely deaf. It is only I who am aware of the minute-crossing of our mutual *Merkwelt*; recognition is but an *Anmerkung* to the limits of individual sensibility. Creek snails, starfish, droning-deaf flies and I are each isolate in the silence of our common but diverse-perceived worlds.

My perceived world is my very own, unlike any other. For a moment it was startling, a consummate coincidental comfort to conceive of deaf creatures collapsed on creek mud, clinging to the pilings, the rocks, crawling lazily up walls, upside down on ceilings all so very close to my typewriter. Mantids were considered deaf before 1986, their escape acrobatics to avoid preying bats an unknown aural mystery. Will I read any day now that a modern day J. Henri Fabre has discovered an ear on a snail, a starfish, a fly or honeybee, somewhere on each singular anatomical structure?

The location of hearing organs in insects can be bizarre. Several species of lacewings and moths have receiving devices, ears of sorts capable of collecting sound in the range of the ultrasonic, on their chests, their mouths, their wings.

These listening receivers are survival detectors sensitive to a bat's echolocating cries. A nocturnal noctuid moth, picking up a bat call, will zigzag out of range of the bat's ultrasonic chirps, or if time is not available, the moth will fold his wings, dropping like a stone. Tiger moths have evolved noisemakers on their chests, a reciprocal irritating grating sound that confuses an approaching bat, interfering with the bat's ability to interpret the information in his returning echoes. Resting by day in caves or tree trunks or clefts in cliffs, some nocturnal moths fly out at twilight issuing ultrasonic cries of their own. *Myotis* flying over the insect world of evening considers from these sounds messages that the moth is a distasteful snack, to be avoided. Why stop for a foul-tasting moth when there are thousands of succulent insects out there?

Some moths and grasshoppers have aural receptors on the base of their abdomens. Mosquitoes hear through their antennae. The tympanic membrane of crickets is on their front legs. A cricket scans his surroundings as he strolls in the underbrush, orienting himself with remarkable "listening" legs, mechanisms so complex he can listen with one leg at a time, receiving vital lifesaving information. Do crickets listen to each other, tuning up their insect orchestra for a summer's night concert, for they are such excellent musicians? In the Orient crickets are often kept as pets, replacing watchdogs, for even while fiddling a steady summer symphony a cricket is listening, his wide acoustic range sensitive even to subsonic ground vibrations. The musicians will cease in unison during a harmonic rendering if someone unknown enters a household. The sudden silence awakens the sleeping family.

Locusts too have their equivalents of our tympanic membrane and eardrums on their legs; the ear of a water bug is within its thorax; and on the soft earth of the warm months a caterpillar responds to sound from the ground, sensing a close predator—a frog, a great blue heron, a small hungry bird. Deathwatch beetles boring through fallen trees create audible tapping messages in their tunnels by pounding their heads against their tunnel walls. Ants with a scraper and rasp mechanism produce sound of such high density or pitch the human ear cannot hear it.

In my personal silent *Umwelt*, here on a northeastern creek, I know it is noisy out there.

It is mid-June. Any day now we will see them, in the fresh tide of early morning, before too many fishermen are out and before most sailors have left marina slips along the creek, headed out to the harbor and the Sound. We will see them at daybreak, sipping our coffee, watching the last of the night herons fly into new-leafed trees, watching red fox and his pups slip into salt-sprayed sedge, disappear in the rising heat of the morning.

The creek will suddenly be alive, underwater volcanoes sending bubbling swirls of spray everywhere, in circles, moving toward us, past us, to the head of the creek, swirling at the end where the town begins, circling back. They will stay, when this happens, in the creek all day, some leaping out of the frothing circles, clear out of their element, the water. It is the annual run of bluefish and snappers, untold thousands of them, all sizes, the larger ones swallowing smaller ones as they fly through the creek. We see them in masses, silvery swift. We speak in whispers. We know they are listening. An engine turned on creates mass havoc as they dive for murkier depths. We know fish can hear.

When they dive they quickly reach sunless depths, as inscrutable as the deeper waters of the near sea, the ocean. This is a commercial creek with the sewage plant outlet at the head of the creek and tugboats daily churning the muddy bottom to obfuscous opacity. Still they can hear us, down there, piled one atop another. Can they see, get about? Some can. Some cannot. It is not sight that aids many fish in navigating dark opaque waters; it is a kind of sixth sense, a "lateral line" along the sides of the fish, a row of tiny sensory organs that respond to the stimuli of near objects, water pressure, sound, not quite an ear but an auditory mechanism that gives a fish information that is part feeling, part hearing. In some fish you can easily spot the lateral line while in others definition is near-invisible, and not only on the sides of the fish body. The lateral line sometimes passes over the head of the fish, branching, surrounding the eyes and gill coverings, ending in the lower jaw. There are pores, small holes, along the lateral line leading to an inner canal, eventually to an auditory area, the location of sensory nerve endings.

In the depths of darkened waters a fish's lateral line

detects and informs him of sunken objects in his path—sunken watercraft and old trees, undersea boulders. The lateral line works in a radar-system fashion. The swimming fish creates water vibrations which bounce off the object, back to him. Blind fish living in deep flooded caves have highly developed inner ear organs as well as highly sensitive lateral lines.

Not only blind fish have inner ears with which to distinguish one sound from another. The inner ears of fish, behind each eye inside the skull, provide equilibrium and balance, as well as additional hearing, in much the same way this faculty is associated with the human ear. A fish's inner ear with its otoliths—chalky calcium-like bone formations found in the inner ears of vertebrates—is of keen interest to scientists studying the striped bass. The otoliths of fish do not change with time, as does most of the bone structure of mammals. There is a permanent memory inherent in the mini-calcareous particles of the fish otoliths containing chemical clues to the food the fish have eaten, the waters inhabited. With the serious decline of the striped bass, scientists want to know just where these fish have been, the quality of those waters, the nutritional and pollution factors.

The three small stone-like bony otoliths provide better hearing to some fish (catfish, carp) than to others (bass, pike). Doesn't matter to the fish—as long as his otoliths are functioning—that some of his brethren have more sophisticated listening devices. It is a wonder only to us that a fish's ears reveal more than its capacity to know his water world: his ear bones hold history.

I cannot wait for the annual run this year. Where have they been—not the smallest, those trying to escape the next largest who in turn flee the larger . . . and larger . . . for the little ones' memory imprints are just beginning, in, of all places, their ears! Thousands are born here in the creek, will wiggle to the surface next week or soon after, their tiny otoliths imprinting the arsenic, thorium, methane, mercury, PCBs, ammonia—radioactivity and other pollutants the EPA has reported—the diffusion of commercial runoff that slips into this creek.

Their history.

16

"Sound swells and recedes; it is intermittent and transient . . .
what we hear is the air itself pushing past a resistance . . . each
sound has a life history which listeners follow by focusing a range
of themselves into an adaptively variable stream. Even when it is
reluctant, hearing is fine-grained, evolving prticipation in what
the source of sound is going through . . . One range of the listener
is the struck and vibrating brass of the bell, while another stands
aside to consider and pass judgment . . . Crooning mother and
listening infant re-create the recent union of their bodies."

DAVE BURROWS,
Sound, Speech, and Music, 1990

 There is music everywhere. Did I notice, day by day, when I had hearing, that every little shop, every restaurant, nearly every passing car seemed to have a radio turned on, a curtain of sound, sometimes soft, sometimes blaring, *there?* Listening, I am alert to what I see, and to a semi-sound world filtered through my hearing aids, half-sounds, the meaning manifest seconds after when defi- nition connects to memory. I remember those electric days many years ago, walking in a trance, wearing my first pair of hearing aids. Each moment was like entering a room known always as sparsely furnished, then coming to the doorway one morning and noticing curtains on the windows, pictures on the walls, giving depth to the room and the life within. How shocking, the knowledge that this extra dimension had always been there. How could I have forgotten? When did such details of everyday life cease to exist for me? Listening when you cannot hear is like that—full of delayed realizations, startling aftershocks, revelations of the just-seconds-ago past while the present slips by unapprehended, missed. Trying to listen in two time dimensions at once—alas! an intricate skill at which I am not too adept.

How quickly we forget things, the ordinary things, the substance of all that surrounds us. We forget to see, to hear, to notice; we forget to listen. Those early hearing aid days, some months after the accident, I was suspended in a continual state of awe and wonder, the air alive with messages that had not reached me in what seemed a long time. I still had some hearing then and I would run on the beach with my dog at the edge of the tide, the subtle splash of water on my toes a water song I would listen to in my head, hours later, incorporating it into a major melodic opus with the sweet rush of the waves, the sharp squawk of the gulls, the crisp crunch of my feet on the sand and reedgrass. How could I not have noticed the emptiness as these sounds disappeared, left me? Something that controls recognition clicked off at some moment, protecting me from consideration of a certain kind of devastation. How wonderful to be reminded, for soon, even with more powerful hearing aids, my water songs would be only memory. Psychologists say that deafness, or a severe hearing loss, acquired after a human being has known hearing, can be the single greatest trauma a person can experience.

It was a magical time. I was fitted with two mini electronic wonders. People said to me, "Oh, they are hardly noticeable," or "If you let your hair grow no one will notice."

Hide them! They were beautiful to me, lovelier than the British Crown Jewels, than the Hope Diamond, than Venus hanging low in the western sky. My hearing aids—even now—are absolute miracles to me. Of course, they are not more beautiful than real hearing . . .

Sound collectors, they were called for hundreds of years, a label that today might be more euphemistically acceptable to people who want a hearing impairment to remain invisible and unaided. At a time when hearing aids are smaller and more acute in their sound-gathering potential than at any time in otoprosthetic history, the fragility of vanity remains embedded in human nature, resisting logic.

And how gather something unseen, an agitation of the air, moving constrictions and attenuations of the unbeheld life-giving element that sustains the world as we know it? How collect the invisible, an intangible that can be felt as discomfort or pain at certain degrees of intensity? With great inventiveness. The evolution of devices to aid deafness is both acoustical and social history. The 1883 London *Catalogue of Acoustical Instruments to Aid the Deaf* notes, in the introduction:

> The ingenuity and taste of the instrument maker are
> required to construct mechanical aids to hearing which

shall combine gracefulness of form and appearance without detracting from their efficiency, for the burden of deafness is great and the sensitiveness of the sufferers should not be wounded by the necessity of announcing their affliction to the public by having to use instruments either unsightly in form or objectionable in color or material.

The assistive devices to aid hearing in this nineteenth-century catalog list natural aids—"placing the hollowed hand behind the ear . . . limiting the entrance of sonorous vibrations to a particular direction," yawning, and learning to "prick or elevate the ears." This last was suggested by a researcher of the time.

Extemporized aids included carrying a parasol or opened umbrella, or wearing a hat of silk or straw. Indoors, positioning oneself near stone or wooden walls "will be found advantageous to the deaf"—something I do all the time, though I have never noticed "touching large pieces of furniture with the finger nails" of any help—a listening aid I should perchance give attention to. Lastly, "a tolerably efficient trumpet may be extemporized by rolling a dry newspaper into the form of a cylindrical tube."

Artificial aids to hearing included a variety of imaginative fanciful apparatus. There were funnels and cones of all sizes and shapes, some quite elegant. I rather like the acoustic cane, individually carved with a sound-collecting protuberance on the side of the cane handle that one rested in one's ear, an inconspicuous device that looked as if, when in use, one were resting one's cane on one's shoulder. Auricles were rather popular, some covered with silk, worn on the head with an adjustable spring between them (like earmuffs), quite popular with women. They could easily be hidden beneath a bouffant hairdo or a bonnet.

Concealed aids were very popular, an acknowledgment by manufacturers of "an inherent delicacy in many persons . . . in advertising their affliction." Sound collectors were ingeniously built into handbags, opera glasses, fans, a beard receptor, and a rather cumbersome brooch-like device that could be attached to a dress, concealed by flowers or a lacy collar. A tube from the bouquet-holder, as this was called, to the ear, gives the secret away.

One of the oldest mechanical hearing aids, the whispering or conversation tube, could be of any length, usually several feet long, a flexible tube of rubber or a metal "slinky" spring covered with a soft fabric, with a piece at one end shaped to fit over or in the ear. The mouthpiece, at the other end, was the sound collector designed in many improvised renditions of the funnel shape. Communication between deaf and hearing was intended to be conducted by the hearing person whispering across the mouthpiece. The author of an 1894 medical textbook advised that too much amplification of the voice, using the tube, "cannot be borne, on account of the generally coincident hyperaesthesia acustica and the giddiness in the head."

The whispering tube reminds me of an electrical device I used for a while several years ago. It was an accessory for my second set of hearing aids. I used it mainly for eating in restaurants. I would place a small amplifier on the table. A microphone hooked onto my companion's shirt or jacket was a sound collector. The amplified sound would radiate, via magnetic waves, to the "telephone pickup" built into my hearing aid. Theoretically, with my hearing aid set to receive magnetic telephone signals, my friend's conversation would be picked up directly by my hearing aid, thus canceling out external restaurant chatter and noise.

We gave it a good try, a wonderful excuse for weekly luncheon appointments at staggered times, testing the level of noise at varying hours. Not a complete failure, it worked poorly, because the mini-microphone on Elsa's lapel, a perfection of modern technology in its near invisibility and remarkable power, picked up more than Elsa's voice. I had so long been out of touch with real hearing, I did not know what many of the collected sounds were. Oh, the air-conditioning, she would say, or that waiter just dropped his tray, or ... There were endless amazements coming into my head.

We gave it up and reverted to our old method—I lipread and request repetition by a known signal if I do not understand what has been said. Perhaps an old whispering tube would have been best, a mechanical device antedating the electronic era of miniature in-the-ear, behind-the-ear sound collectors.

I lost my hearing rapidly after the accident. There was the big loss, all at once, and then a period of some years as the little that was left diminished. I would say to my audiologist at yearly checkups, "I think there is wax in my ears," or

"Something is wrong with my aids. I cannot seem to turn them high enough."

Isolation was always there. Things were happening around me and I did not react, did not know, until someone would tell me. In a rare moment of truth I admitted, one day, that when I did hear a sound, a noise, a something, I had to think carefully, trying to identify what it was I was hearing. Sound definition was leaving me. And worse—when I did hear something, I could not tell what direction it was coming from. Hearing difficulty was one thing; deaf—and all that word implied—was another. I skipped that year's checkup. I already had hearing aids. What else could be done?

The following year I did go for an audiological examination. I was told exactly what I expected to hear: I had very little hearing left. It was suggested I have a hearing aid evaluation which would determine if newer, more sophisticated models would be helpful.

Twice I rescheduled the appointment. The day I finally appeared was cold and damp, as bleak as my mood. The audiologist had studied the results of my recent testing. She had narrowed down the possibilities. There were two new hearing aids she felt would improve my awareness and sound definition. Hearing aids, at their very best, do not restore hearing, but they can maximize the hearing a person still has. A hearing aid amplifies sound, often imperfectly. The more advanced the technology, the better the quality of the information received by the listening hearing aid wearer. I had forgotten the ordinary ongoing noises of life. I was so unprepared for that afternoon.

Both models were marvelous, one more helpful. "Sounds like some children are having fun in the hall": my first words, said in stunned surprise. The large offices of the New York League for the Hard of Hearing, devoted to the needs of people like myself, were usually extraordinarily quiet, no matter how crowded. I forgot this was only *my* perception of things.

"Oh . . . those children have been playing out there for the whole hour you have been in this room." My audiologist suggested I take a brief walk, wander the halls, the offices, step into any room I wished and just listen. Listen!

Always, I think I *am* listening. It involves so much more than stretching the ability of my ears. Listening has become an aching attempt to comprehend at least some of the sounds, the meanings of life around me. Listening has meant hope that communication with whoever is there at the moment will be possible.

The first thing I noticed was music. Low radios hummed in every small alcove, masking what had always seemed austere surroundings. The waiting room was noisy. The flip of a magazine page was jolting, explosive, a firecracker stunning my sensibilities. Sound was everywhere. I did not understand what all of it was . . . but it *was* . . . heard . . . it was sound!

I returned to the little room of the testing, an immense sadness muting my voice to a whisper. "There is a whole world out there." I said. "How is it possible I did not know . . . forgot . . . and how . . . how can I ever hope to have access to that world?" I knew what those wonderful hearing aids cost. I had asked right away. I was unemployed and had insurmountable debts. I cried all the way home.

It was cold and dark early, January. I opened the door to my houseboat, stepping inside. Sheena signaled to me that the telephone was ringing, a telephone especially adapted for my use. It was Jack Lee, an old friend, a devoted member of the local Lions Club, a man who had spent much of his life working with the Lions and their projects that aid the handicapped, especially the blind. He was saying something about the Lions wanting to get more involved in projects for the hearing impaired. "Tell me," he asked, "do you need new hearing aids? My group would like to do something for you . . ."

I had not yet taken off my coat. The wind was rocking the boat. I said, "Jack . . . could you please repeat that slowly? You know I cannot hear too well . . . " This Lions group knew me. We had worked together on fund-raising activities when I was a librarian for the handicapped ten years before.

The ordinary moments of life nine years ago became pure adventure. I was not used to all the murmurs of living around me. Things most people accept, never think about, startled me with their *thereness*, their closeness, sharp intrusions on the silence I was used to. For instance, a Sunday. I flick my mini-switches to "on." The loudspeaker of the marina several hundred yards away is blaring an announcement. After listening to them all week I am learning to decipher some words. I had lived in that boatyard on the good ship *Bette Anne* for over three years. I never knew there was a loudspeaker so nearby, audible to everyone but me.

What else came through? At six o'clock one morning a couple on the boat next to me had a feisty exchange on who would go out for the newspaper. And I noticed when my dog barked she was greeted by a canine from a nearby craft. Did that dog always answer her? Probably. Since it is Sunday I tune out the world by a simple flick to "off." The Sunday traffic of people and motoring crowds is annoying. Others complain. I alone have supreme options.

In my *chosen* moments of complete silence, I recalled the electrifying moment, that morning my new hearing aids arrived by registered mail, a small box, truly a cornucopia I could not wait to open. A note was attached: "The Melville [New York] Lions Club is honored to have had the opportunity to have improved the quality of your life." Trembling I tore off the wrapping. Their insides were quite different than those of my old hearing aids. These new aids were tiny computer terminals, a miracle of small elements arranged in an intricate, inscrutable design. I had to bring them to my audiologist, who tuned them in to my world.

Then for a time there was music in my home, flowing softly across the shallow waters that surrounded *Bette Anne*. I would take out a special attachment that connected my cassette player to my new hearing aids, my secret connection to a world long missed. I touched the cassettes. I had not heard them for such a long time. Yes . . . for a while . . . there really was music everywhere.

The old mechanical sound collectors had a romantic éclat. I can see myself quivering a fan with a hidden sound collector as Elsa and I order Hunan lamb or Lake Tung-Ting shrimp, extra spicy. I doubt that I would have hidden a sound collector in my wild hair or my muff . . . but in my cane, yes, certainly, a cane surely that held secretly, too, a hidden vial of brandy, a sip for the moments of stress.

The days of mechanical hearing aids ended in the early twentieth century. Carbon-type and vacuum tube electrical aids provided amplification. The invention of the transistor in 1947 was the beginning of a new era. The modern hearing aid, its small size and shape established by 1953, could now, with digital electronics, be individually programmed.

I am wearing my third set of hearing aids, digital wonders. I do not hear birds or the splash of my feet in the evening surf; or the geese hawking into our harbor, their evening haven; or the neighboring canine or the exchange between him and Sheena. The radio is fuzzy and I am never sure of the weather reports; but conversation is clearer . . . though disconnected, since I do not hear every word. In a one-to-one dialogue, assisted by lipreading, I enjoy conversation about as efficiently as I would with a whispering tube. Just less visible. The new hearing aids lend unexpected surprises, a sound collected that is quite extraordinary, a puzzlement, a mystery, decoded eventually by a hearing person, clarified as something known, once.

I read about new wonders to come . . . already here, but hardly marketable. We have learned to think small. The new digital aids, with all their exceptional refinements, several microphones, components that produce reduction in background noise far beyond current single-microphone designs, cannot yet be packaged in any but a body-worn unit, something we have assumed technology has surpassed. "It is anticipated," said one report, "that with continued progress in the microminiaturization of digital circuit chips, the necessary components for a digital hearing aid will become small enough for a practical ear level or all-in-the-ear unit to be developed in the near future."

I want those new wonders now! Want to clip on that body unit, wired to my ears, pick up *who knows!* the screech of a foraging great blue heron. I want to listen to whatever is out there without having to anatomize my hearing aids' components; technology does not grasp me; hearing—however it happens—does.

Serendipity—coming upon wonderful things accidentally— stayed with me in 1984 (a year that included negotiating the low tide ramp and the dock for four months in a leg cast and crutches, three additional months in an arm cast, and the sinking of the good ship *Bette Anne*). Shortly after receiving my new hearing aids from the Melville Lions, I walked into an auto parts store for some spark plugs for my ailing, elderly, much-loved fourteen-year-old Chevy convertible. The owner was a member of the Huntington Lions Club, a village adjacent to Melville. Joe said, "Hannah . . . we're get-

ting into the hearing field too. It's amazing you're here . . .
I'm supposed to call you today . . . We know about the hearing aids . . . what else could you use?"

Dare I tell him . . . ? It was such a terrible year. The list
of things I wanted was long. I had lost most of my belongings and all electrical appliances when my home sank in a
freak storm. It was raised the same night by neighboring
liveaboards, and I was still living aboard. It was where I
wanted to be.

Yes, the list was very long. I knew what I wanted, something that topped the list even before the sinking.

I wanted a TDD—a telecommunications device for the
deaf—a telephone system that would enable me to type out
telephone calls and receive typed telephone communications.
The kind of communication that exists today with state
relay systems did not exist then, but there were enough people I knew, services I was aware of that had TDDs to assure
me it would soften the difficulties I was having even with
amplified telephone attachments.

I asked Joe for a TDD . . . so excited by his affirmative
response that I left his shop without my spark plugs.

The Huntington Lions invited me to a dinner meeting,
presenting their gift to me. With Sheena lying across my
toes (snacking on crumbs on the floor), I spoke to them.
Someone taped my unintended speech, typing it out for me:

> Once upon a time a woman spoke. Her voice, echoing in
> the room, was a miracle in itself. "The sound of the voice,"
> she said, "brings language, sets thoughts astir . . . ours is not
> the silence that soothes the weary senses; it is the inhuman

silence which severs and estranges . . . a silence which isolates."

Helen Keller was expressing what communication meant to her, what it was like to live without it, what it was to be cut off in a sensory way from everything around you. She recalled her younger self, a wild blind-deaf child, her mind a fertile but fallow field, waiting.

I am in wonder of Helen Keller, the largeness of her internal vision. She spoke of the differences of her two handicaps. "The problems of deafness are more complex . . . than those of blindness. Deafness is a much worse misfortune because of the loss of that vital stimulus—the sound of the voice."

I know it is almost beyond imagining for you to grasp the meaning of my words when I say, "I am deaf." My eyeglasses tell you my vision is not perfect. The cast on my arm suggests a recent mishap. Nothing about me tells you my world is quiet. And I cannot tell you what my world is like. How can you close your ears?

For seven years I lived without a telephone. It was easier. Last year, succumbing to the demands of children, family, friends, editors, I reconnected to the real world, even though my hearing had diminished to a profound loss. I have an answering machine, the messages received by it unintelligible to me. Someone helps me sort out the meanings.

The telephone did not mean freedom for me. I soon realized that if my telephone was to be a communication system for me—"set thoughts astir"—I would need a telecommunication device for the deaf, a TDD. Connected to my ordinary telephone I could type or speak my part of the conversation, and receive a printed answer.

How can I thank you? Emerson once said, "A gift is a portion of thyself." You have given me a precious gift—a reconnection with the immediacy of spontaneous conversation—and independence. I shall think of you often . . . to each Lion . . . I send a hug . . .

In the autumn of 1983, photographs of President Ronald Reagan in profile appeared in newspapers, a small in-the-ear hearing aid resting in his right ear. Mr. Reagan, at age seventy-two, had expressed the hope, according to a spokesman, "that his wearing a hearing aid publicly would set an example for others who might be reluctant to use one."

Set an example!!!! The *New York Times* news item continues, reporting that "Mr. Reagan's hearing problems date from the 1930s, when a .38-caliber pistol was fired near his right ear while he was acting in a movie." *Newsday* stated, in a September 8, 1983, article, that "the President has had trouble hearing questions and other conversation for several years. During the 1980 presidential campaign his aides discussed whether to have him wear a hearing aid, and decided against it because it would remind voters of his age."

What could an incensed deaf writer do? I wrote a letter to the editor that appeared in the *Chicago Tribune* (October 16, 1983):

MR. REAGAN, ARE YOU LISTENING?

Dear President Reagan,

I must thank you. Because of news items I ripped from newspapers recently, I did something I have been talking about for years: I painted my hearing aids pink . . .

My hearing aids, dear President, have always been beautiful to me, even as recently as yesterday, when they were still the color tan, the color of indecision. They represent a dimension of life to me, a sense dimension I am missing: Sound.

I see, too, from the news items, that we have other similar problems.

We both stumble through life a little less with our aids to vision, you with your contact lenses, I with my constantly misplaced eyeglasses. If I ever suspect that imminently I will be cast ashore on a desert island I shall be certain my survival equipment contains several extra pairs of glasses, extra hearing aids, and an infinite supply of batteries. How can I forage for food or be aware of wild beasts without them? But then . . . being cast ashore, being bereft of ordinary communication, is not something a President, or public figure, has often had to think about. No wonder you waited fifty years to get a hearing aid. You never had to be alone.

According to the news reports, your hearing loss occurred in the 1930s. According to the same reports, you discussed with your aides whether or not to allow your hearing to be improved by a hearing aid because it would remind voters of your age. I can see that it would imply to your public that you have imperfections, like most of us.

I cannot remember Franklin Delano Roosevelt hiding his wheelchair. Instead he inspired the wheelchair-walkers of this world to stand on their own two wheels. Recently, when I discovered that the very little hearing I have left would probably leave me soon, I was paralyzed with fear, with the isolation I already know. "So what!" my feisty sister said to me. "Who in the world can stand on their own two ears?"

We have another thing in common, dear President. I, too, am hearing impaired due to an accident. Mine was twelve years ago, when I was thirty-nine. It has changed the direction of my life ... but to wait fifty years to improve things??

I would be proud to have a president who flaunts a hearing aid. What a place of power to advertise the small wonders of modern life! I can see, with a little promotion, how hearing aids could become more popular than earrings. All those people who are reluctant, afraid of an image, who put off (as apparently you yourself) enhancing of their lives for years, think how much you could have influenced them!

But alas, it is true. You know it yourself. Vanity was more overwhelming, more overpowering than truth, than need, than sound, than touch. For a hearing aid really is one thing: touch.

As it happens, dear President, I painted my two hearing aids with a pink Magic Marker. It is rubbing off already as I fondle them. Perhaps if I use nail polish ... You see, it is very important. There are millions of people out there, still years away from their seventies, who need just a little encouragement to know it really is all right, that not-hear-ing-all-that-well, though scary and inconvenient, is not the end of the world. I know they need someone to shout for them. I just wish that you had.

Nothing is final. Not in scientific revelation or human discovery of any kind. It has been thought, until recently, that the upper range of human hearing—when auditory intake is at perfection—is at 20,000 hertz per second, the point at which sound becomes ultrasound, beyond the range of human hearing.

In July 1991, the journal *Science* had a remarkable report entitled "Human Ultrasonic Speech Perception," which included the following:

Bone-conducted ultrasonic hearing has been found capable of supporting frequency discrimination and speech detection in normal, older-hearing-impaired, and profoundly deaf human subjects. When speech signals were modulated into the ultrasonic range, listening to words resulted in the clear perception of the speech stimuli and not a sense of high-frequency vibration. These data suggest that ultrasonic bone conduction hearing has potential as an alternative communication channel in the rehabilitation of hearing disorders.

Apparently, when the conditions are right (knock wood ... that is, knock skull), language can be understood in the elite ranges of the ultrasonic by hearing as well as deafened people. The catch is that the stimuli, the open-sesame to the ultrasonic, depends on bone conduction. "Ultrasonic hearing may," notes the article, "... be capable of serving as a viable alternative communication channel ... for individuals with varying degrees of hearing loss."

Thus the thought-to-be ultimate of digital computerized hearing aids has barely been touched. The acoustical discoveries propose the possibility of an auditory organ other than the cochlea "which detects the sounds of everyday life ... [suggesting] a new approach for designing devices to help those who can hear little or nothing in normal audio ranges" (*New York Times*, July 5, 1991). This, too, was a serendipitous discovery.

Dr. Martin L. Lenhardt was attempting to repel endangered sea turtles from beaches to enhance their chance for survival. Using ultrasonic alarms Dr. Lenhardt and his colleagues discerned "considerable modulations and tonal differences in frequencies supposedly way above [their] hearing

capacity, in the range of 30,000 cycles a second and beyond."
They were using a device attached to the head which had the
capability of vibrating rapidly in response to sound. "You
perceive the vibrations as sound," Dr. Lenhardt said, when
the device vibrated at high frequencies. Dr. Lenhardt and his
researchers discovered that words conducted ultrasonically
through their vibrating mechanism were readily understood.
The bones in the head, when vibrated by ultrasonic noises,
did not deliver the "monotonous squeals" expected: "What
amazed me," Dr. Lenhardt stated, was that "when I first
heard it, it sounded like speech."

The possible uses of this phenomenon are still in the
experimental stage. Dr. Lenhardt is focusing on the saccule, an
organ in the inner ear, a minuscule gel-filled sac usually
thought of as significant in maintaining balance. Vibrating
waves from the bones in the skull running through the saccule
perhaps travel to the brain, bypassing the cochlea (heretofore
considered the receiver of sound through which acoustic messages are sent to the brain), suggesting marvels of the future
for the deaf and hearing impaired. Bone-conducted ultrasonic
stimulation "may provide an alternative therapeutic approach
for the rehabilitation of severe hearing loss." The researchers
are thinking small, as befits almost-twenty-first-century
sleuths of the scientific. They hope, notes the *New York Times*,
to "eventually have a little patch the size of a quarter that can
be taped to the neck to translate normal speech into ultrasonic tones for those who are partly or wholly deaf."

I will want mine visible. I will paint it pink ... never
liked turtlenecks anyway.

17

". . . I close my eyes, and the planet is auditory only: tree branches twist into tubas and saxes, are caught by large hands that press down valves, and everywhere on this ranch I hear feral music—ghostly tunes made not by animals gone wild but by grasses, sagebrush, and fence wire singing . . ."

GRETEL EHRLICH,
Island, the Universe, Home, 1991

 My world is alive with presence—with vibrations, swish, movement—a silent visual feast. I listen for it in the half-dark of near morning as Harvey and I sip fresh ground coffee in the pilothouse of our home, the good ship *Haimish*, the heat of an incipient new day rising in deepening pink light. We are watching the creatures of early light—evanescent night herons flitting off to tangled trees, cormorants standing on an old submerged tire in the shallows, scalloped wings outspread, drying; great blue herons, tall white egrets stabbing shoal waters; low-flying gulls gliding on unseen thermals; the exotic rapturous flight of a vast blur of red-winged blackbirds simultaneously settling in a single tree. Sandpipers and killdeer skitter on wet sand at the lapping edge of the tide; geese glide out of the reedgrass where they have spent the night; our swans and mallards swim toward us for morning snacks we will toss out, while one mallard couple waddles across the roof of my office, our houseboat, the *Bette Anne*. Our youngest cat, Elijah, on the dock between the two boats is stalking the complacent roofed couple. The female is chattering away, the male at her side silent, beak closed. "A musician," Harvey says, excited, "could create a composition, a musical morning dance of the birds . . . and another on their eternal conversation."

I watch our winter and summer flyers, cognizant of their choreography, the idiosyncratic dance of each, singular, significant within each species, their movements part of their communication system. I am reminded of Alexander Graham Bell's wife, Mabel, a deaf lipreader taught in the oralist tradition that forbade sign language. Her granddaughter said: "It always made a tremendous impression on me . . . the theme . . . the sound and the silence. He was always trying to re-create sound for her and she was always trying to understand that sound . . . she couldn't remember sound . . . and always when we would walk with them, he was always telling her the sound he heard . . . a cow bell or whatever it was."

The voices of birds would be lost to me were it not for Harvey's description of their individual vocalizations, kindling memory with words, reminding me that sound is present with language that separates bird from bird.

Running my fingers over imaginary piano keys I compose

a "Dance of the Morning Birds"—an étude, an arabesque, a sprightly melody of my morning scene, impassioned—heard as a function of memory, a receiving of images anew.

Will such sensitivity of mind engender me with powers to sense and capture the ineluctable, the unexpected that will surely appear in my life?

I must know . . . for it is lack of sensitivity of a special kind that I have been engulfed in for many months, for over a year. When a vital sense has gone askew, when a mishap occurs, when part of our personal radar system with which we perceive the world becomes lost to us—how desperately we need to know that empathy, understanding, recognition of our altered perspective has, in the process of human concern, become part of "out there"—an inherent part of the world we touch, the people we meet.

A LAW IS A LAW IS NOT A LAW . . . with apologies to Gertrude Stein.

It is a simple statement, nearly invisible in the cumbersome guide of many volumes comprising New York State's judicial statutes. A copy of it is always in my wallet, crunched next to my library card, my driver's license, and the photo ID of Sheena and me issued by the Guide Dog Foundation of Smithtown (New York), an ID which tells the world we are a legal couple—hearing guide dog and person with impaired hearing. Yes, New York State Civil Rights Statute Article 4-B, Sections a-c, has always been a quiescent sleeping safeguard to me—**THE LAW**—something to show, along with our guide dog ID, to anyone questioning Sheena's right to be with me in a public place.

And so it was, a dormant defender of my civil rights.

Until March 6, 1991, the day I precipitated a legal action invoking this law, pressing a claim of abuse of my civil rights. To date, nearly three years later—the New York State judicial system has failed to prosecute two violations of Article 4-B, which reads in part:

> No person shall be denied admittance to and/or the equal use of and enjoyment of any public facility solely because said person is blind or deaf or because said person is blind or deaf and is accompanied by a guide dog (47:1).

It has happened before during the twelve years we have lived and traveled together, the questioning of the propriety of my companion appearing with me in public buildings, restaurants, educational facilities, office buildings, airplanes, theaters, libraries—but never have we been so verbally assaulted by such witless brutality, such savage indifference to my deafness, as Sheena and I were subjected to on March 6, 1991, by the director of a public library in Long Island, New York.

On March 6, I was using the reference section of this library, something I had been doing frequently for the four years I had lived in this community, when I was asked to remove my animal from the premises. The library director arbitrarily rejected the identification card always with me which states that Sheena is a licensed hearing ear guide dog, one of about 2,000 in the country, specifically trained for the needs of people with hearing loss. Our ID has carried us across the country, Sheena lying at my feet in the passenger section of any airplane; she is not denied access to restaurants or hospitals (recently finding the treadmill in the Glen Cove Hospital stress test lab much more fun than I did), and Sheena has never been denied access to libraries anywhere.

Rejecting our ID as authentic, the library director refused, too, to glance at the New York State Civil Rights Statute which I plucked from a library shelf and opened to the appropriate page.

I wrote to the president of the board of trustees immediately following this incident, expecting (naïvely, perhaps) an immediate response. I am still waiting—and the incident was repeated two weeks later, on March 19, 1991.

Good things—and one shocking thing—began to happen. I had sent copies of my letter to the board of trustees to several state legal agencies and to the editors of several newspapers. Newspapers quickly found deaf-woman-with-unwanted-canine a great human interest item. Sheena posed poignant and attentive for front- and near-front-page news fame.

My case then rested until December 1991 with the office of the attorney general, in its various domains in Albany, Hempstead, and New York City. Month after month I was told the attorney general's office was trying to decide if indeed they were the agency to administer my complaint. Here is a law, with penalties for its violation, and no one seemed to know who was responsible for prosecuting it!

The newspaper stories engendered countless wonderful

letters—offers to have disastrous things done to the library director; one offer of marriage ("I will take good care of Sheena . . . call me at II P.M., no earlier, no later . . . tell me how tall you are"); several promises of cures for my deafness for unspecified but hinted-at sums; and, oh-very-best, a TTY call from Loretta H. Murray, Esq., a deaf lawyer, offering to wrestle with my case and ensure that New York State confront and prosecute violations of a law in the compilation of its statutes.

I am often asked, Why are you bothering with this? I remember March 6; the library director pursued Sheena and me relentlessly from one part of the library to another as I researched the material I was looking for, trying to ignore him, refusing to be evicted. A crowd gathered, following us. He said he did not believe my deafness. ("You have not convinced me of your need for that . . . that animal.")

I have a disability, one that is invisible. The damage to the nerves in my ears leaves my lack of ability to receive and comprehend sound on an audiological level labeled profound loss. My major disability is not my deafness; it is that I speak well, am an excellent lipreader. The only clues that might alert an astute observer that something is amiss in my communication system are my hearing aids and the fact that I am always accompanied by a dog.

Libraries are central to my life. I have lived in libraries long before writing and research became my profession. In fact, I *am* a librarian, one who established and directed the Suffolk County, New York, "Reading for the Handicapped" program, an arm of the Library of Congress. For years I have given seminars and talks to inform service organizations (such as libraries) of the rights, the lives of people with disabilities. How ironic that I should become a prominent example of the abuse of such rights.

For my work Sheena and I pursue libraries everywhere. The Acoustical Society of America (Woodbury, New York) had no difficulty welcoming us into its august quarters for a morning's work. Adelphi University's science library gives us time, free access to obscure periodicals. And more than once, after work in Hofstra University's library, Sheena and I have been invited to lunch in the faculty dining room.

"Let the shameful walls of exclusion come tumbling down," President George Bush commented in July 1990, shortly after signing into law the Americans with Disabilities Act (ADA). "Every man, woman and child with a disability can now pass through a once-closed door to a bright new era of equality, independence and freedom." Words this library director, and too many others in and out of legal chambers, never bothered to read, do not care to know.

I am one of the 24 million persons with hearing loss the ADA has already begun to affect since its implementation in January 1992. Will this law effectively mitigate the need for us to ask for our civil rights? Will it lessen the requirement of a militant response if we want to claim such rights? Will professional people continue to ignore our wanting to be part of ordinary—and extraordinary—life?

Communication in my world is often a chancy thing, a fuzziness, a blur I struggle to dissipate to intuit what is happening. The director of this library, I imagine, hears the call of wild winds, the cry of a child, the songs of birds, the soft patter of rain. I know he cannot hear the plunging, the crushing of a human heart he has just stepped on in the officious efficiency of performing his job.

I am horrified to realize that a public employee is unaware of the rights of people with disabilities. He demonstrated how poorly qualified some civil employees are—perchance through mere lack of understanding—to give even the most basic adequate service to a community as diversified as this city.

I am even more dismayed to see that he is supported—if only by sheer indifference—by a legal system that does not act to enforce laws it has sworn to defend. What hope for the enforcement of the ADA is there, on the national level, when such ennui exists, indeed thrives, on the state level?

How many state laws exist that no one has challenged . . . or given up challenging in the process because no office has been assigned to administer their infractions? And why pursue such infractions when even the attorney general of the state has relinquished responsibility?

My complaint was a serious one. I wanted it recognized, a step toward educating the public to the invisible condition of people whose ability to hear has been diminished, perhaps this sense so missing that a coherent grasp of sound and speech just does not occur.

For a year I thought we would meet in court, the library, Sheena and I, and dear Loretta, my attorney, who has more faith in the plodding progress of the law than do I. Sheena could not wait to place her paw on a Bible before testifying.

In October 1991, representatives of the New York State attorney general's office in Manhattan met briefly with Sheena and me, and my attorney. They had met separately with library officials and their attorney the week before. The assistant district attorneys asked me what I wanted, what kind of conclusion was I seeking.

I had two interests in mind, I told them: a public apology; and I wanted the library to commence an educational program for employees and the community, one that would ease communication and establish outreach contact with the disabled community in the city of Glen Cove. I had created and participated in such programs; I knew they could be powerful and effective.

On December 20, 1991, my attorney received notice from the attorney general's office: "We have concluded that our office lacks statutory authority to pursue Ms. Merker's complaint."

At the same time, we received from the library's attorney a release for me to sign (relinquishing all current and future charges), and a copy of the apology the library would issue upon receipt of the signed release, which reads, in part:

> While confident that neither the library nor its employees or officials committed any wrongdoing, the Board of Trustees of the Glen Cove Public Library sincerely regrets any perceived hardship you may have felt as a result of the events which transpired on March 6, 1991 . . .

My case became a moot point as of January 26, 1992. Much of the ADA which became effective that day pertains to the needs of the estimated 24 million people with hearing loss in the United States. Will federal offices give credence to complaints of violations, implementing, enforcing our civil rights?

We should select a day—soon—when all the guide dogs on Long Island—across the country—will walk into public places with their persons . . .

all at once . . .

sniffing, savoring new smells . . .

nostrils aquiver . . .

a unanimous declaration to be recognized . . .

My library . . . anyguidedog ? ? ? ? ?

AFTERWORD

"*Language. I loved it. And for a long time I would think of myself, of my whole body, as an ear.*"

MAYA ANGELOU,
New York Times, January 20, 1993

 Most of the estimated 24 million deaf, hearing impaired, and speech impaired persons in the United States were born with perfect or near-perfect hearing. Most of us were born listening creatures. The majority of us living now in silent and semi-silent worlds leapt into the cacophony of modern life hearing . . . listening. Most of us remember knowing sound, at one time . . .

If we have had hearing for many years, we may still have speech, often excellent articulation, as opposed to the atonal voice of someone born deaf, or deafened in early life. Yet we are, in some respects, part of the same world; we are deaf by audiological standards, or so hearing impaired that our retrieval and comprehension of ordinary conversation is severely restricted ... a guessing game of sorts, rarely won. Somewhere along our timeline an illness, an accident, an unexplained genie landing upon us has diminished our sense of sound. Our known world has changed significantly, ultimately on a lone intimate level. Our intelligence grasps at mere phrases of speech, where conversation is a fluid interacting process, producing laughter and repartée, leaving many of us, those without a friendly interpreter, on the fringe of thinking at any ordinary moment.

Many of us wear hearing aids, love the limited gift they give us; additional, never complete, understanding. Some of us are excellent lipreaders, which means we comprehend words here and there, 50 percent—usually less—of a conversation with wild wonderful guesses for the rest. And some of us have a walking pair of ears at our left side at all times, a member of an elite but growing troop of four-footed canine creatures trained to be our ears.

One day years ago, while I worked at the reference desk of the Huntington (New York) Public Library, a Labrador retriever placed his damp nose on my desk, a paw on my knee, insisting I speak to his person who was holding a malfunctioning talking book machine. Where could I get his machine fixed ... and more pressing ... how would he read while it was under repair? Abner (the dog, a perfect gentleman) sniffed my feet thoroughly, inhaling the aroma of Barney, my boxer, who, though I did not know it at the time, would soon become my first hearing guide dog.

Abner's person sat down in the easy chair I kept by my desk while I tried to track down a local representative of the Telephone Pioneers of America, an organization of retired telephone company employees long dedicated to repairing the equipment that the blind use to "read." I also arranged for this avid reader to have another machine sent to him, a loaner. (As it happens he and Abner were in the middle of *Lolita* and were indeed distressed at the technological failure that had brought their listening to a halt.)

I walked them to the door, a Pied-Piper-following of children at our heels. Abner greeted them all, a lick here, a tail wag there ... my colleagues, the other librarians, the superb staff at the circulation desk of this fine library seemed rather glad to be behind the counter. There was silence as Abner's person paused at the door, one hand grasping Abner's harness, the other reaching delicately toward me. He found me, sightless eyes staring over my shoulder, his free hand on my sleeve inching its way up to my shoulder, my neck, my cheek. "Thank you," he said, a smile illuminating his whole face. Quickly, before either he or I had time to think, he leaned over to where his light fingers rested on my face, kissing my cheek. "Shall I call a taxi for you?" I asked, my voice hushed and hoarse with unexplained feelings. He deferred the taxi, preferring to walk. It was only a mile to his home and Abner was familiar with several alternate routes. He'd let Abner decide.

Glancing back at the library I realized what I had never

given thought to before—how people fear the unknown. Blindness was an unknown—or worse yet—a known no one wanted to think about, get close to, touch. Had I visually dissolved all those no-nos in a confrontation that took only brief minutes?

I told our staff about Helen Keller writing to Mabel Bell from Radcliffe after a visit with Alexander and Mabel Bell in their Nova Scotia home: ". . . the smell of the ocean," she wrote, "and the fragrance of the pines have followed me to Cambridge and linger about like a benediction." The essence of the Bells' home known, intuited, a sensory perception beyond the reality of failed senses. The remarkable sensitivity, the poetic sensibility of Helen Keller's awareness of her surrounding world were perceptions discerned from her openness, her curiosity about life. Alexander Bell's experiments, her participation in some of them, excited her interest in the scientific: "one day he placed her hand on a telephone pole and asked what it meant to her, then explained that the wires it carried sang of life and death, war and finance, fear and joy, failure and success, that they pierced the barriers of space and touched mind to mind throughout the world."

Helen Keller, in her sightlessness, her soundlessness, embraced the world of seeing and hearing. Mabel Bell denied the world of silence, insisting on visual communication, writing near the end of her life: "I shrink from any reference to my disability and won't be seen in public with another deaf person." Mabel's speech was poorly understood by most outside her immediate family and close friends. Last night, walking near midnight under a crescent moon, giving Sheena her last amble of the day, Harvey and I talked in the darkened boatyard, our conversation interspersed with comfortable pauses beneath overhead lights so I could see what he was saying and respond to it. He could hear me in the dark; it was I who needed the light, dependent on visual cues for listening, for comprehension. Once at a dinner party, about 100 years ago, Alexander Graham Bell asked a friend to walk Mabel home while he kept another appointment. The guest knew the rhythm the conversation would take: Mabel would chat in the dark of the evening, waiting under each street lamp for her escort's response, adamant always that communication seem effortless, ordinary.

In Susan Schaller's recent book, *A Man Without Words*, she describes the frustrations, the excitement of a teacher faced with an educational challenge that had few precedents, nearly no maps at all to follow. She is trying to give words, thoughts, ideas, concepts . . . the means to express them . . . to a twenty-seven-year-old languageless man:

> I wondered what kept us working . . . what pushed us every morning to face each other? . . . When I look back I don't recall the student Ildefonso, but Ildefonso my friend. As friends, we pushed each other to explore . . . we knew we were involved in an adventure together . . . A new friendship can sometimes cause one to feel that life is happening for the first time. Ildefonso and I experienced this newness and the challenge of rethinking Everything.

That is what education is—the continual "challenge of rethinking Everything." The best learning experiences I have had, in and out of academic life, both as student and teacher, have been those that meant exploration—not just research; exploration of ideas and ways to implement them; presenting the known when faced with seemingly impossible obstacles (like trying to teach English composition to a class of eighteen college students, fourteen of whom spoke little or no English—nothing in my varied career had prepared me for this).

The new challenge becomes an exploration of self, a quest for a beginning, and, in my personal case with this class, how to communicate—how to listen to each other, comprehend each other, understand each other.

Lipreading which I rely on was obviously going to be useless until I became more familiar with my students and their individual ways of speaking. Henry Kisor describes the chanciness of lipreading in *What's That Pig Outdoors: A Memoir of Deafness:*

> Conversations among more than three or four people are nearly impossible for even highly skilled lipreaders to follow. It takes a few moments to catch the rhythm and sense of one person's words . . . we never catch up, falling further and further behind as our minds slowly make sense of what we're seeing. Once in a while the light of understanding will shine upon us long after the talk has passed to another topic.

Kisor calls himself "a member of a minority within a minority: I am what is called an 'oralist.' That is, I depend wholly on spoken language and lipreading, however imperfect they might be, to help me live and work in a hearing world. I do not know sign language at all." Book editor and columnist for the *Chicago Sun-Times,* Kisor has been deaf from an illness since the age of three.

> What did take root was a love for the way words sounded. I could not, of course, hear them—the auditory spectrum was beyond my competence. But words have definite and distinct vibrations and I could roll them across my tongue, feeling how they thrummed on my throat, cheeks, teeth, lips, and nose. Nose. Knows. The nose knows. The *nnozze knowzz.* My nostrils would resonate with each "n," my lips with each "o." The "z" brought forth a delicious low buzz on the tips of the front teeth. All this I could "hear" on the tympanum of my mind.

So, too, at this moment I "hear" the gale winds that have been rocking this good ship for nearly four days. In the rocking a loud thump draws me to a port window, a vibration under my feet strong enough for me to label it "loud." Boat fenders protect us, pounding into the dock, a sound "heard" through memory of feeling associated with the impact of surrounding phenomena—the swirling current inches from the bow, the wind-rippled crested waters, the gulls flying backward.

I do not actually "hear" all this, in the sense that sound translates to meaning for a hearing person. I "hear" the wild wind vividly, an instant recall, triggered by instantaneously translated knowing of vibrations and visual sightings. Listening I know—there it is, the invisible air pushing our mast easterly, leaning over us; there it is, the slap of gale-pushed waters, visible in white-rising spume and a stretch of white-surfaced sea splashing across the beach; there it is, in the screech of a herring gull atop a near piling, his beak opening and shutting emitting high-pitched shrieks I cannot hear, yet resonant to me. Mabel Bell always positively would say she could feel and hear sound and silence.

While my contention with my local library hung in the limbo of indecision in the office of the New York State attorney general, anticipating their questions concerning the resolution of the case I wrote three education papers—suggestions for ongoing education and outreach programs to initiate and conduct in this community. Suggestions and programs I knew worked, created eager response and mutuality of feeling. I had used such programs, seen the excitement they generated, the community interaction that precipitated genuine insight into the lives of the handicapped. The recognition of universal humanness that disseminates fear—the ebbing of guarded tensions evident among our employees after my afternoon with Abner and his person—were part of the issues I wrote about. I described what happened at the Huntington Public Library after that day—to the staff and the community (both abled and disabled)—as I began the process to establish Huntington as a subregional division of the Library of Congress's Division for the Visually and Physically Handicapped.

Did they listen—those trustees of my community library, those officials in the office of the attorney general—to the deafening sound of the kinetic energy of community response as they read my brief papers, old possibilities that could be created anew?

Did they even read them?

Last year in a small town in the hills rising northeast of San Francisco, I sat in my son's living room, at the edge of a luncheon meeting of about twenty people, a committee preparing a discussion panel to be presented at their local library. My son brought out sandwiches, salads, deftly maneuvering platters while dragging recalcitrant long legs across the room with his Canadian crutches—the kind that clip onto one's upper arms (ah ... ! the insidious, relentless, progressive claim on his body by multiple sclerosis ...).

His wheelchair was in constant use, friends taking turns sailing across the long room to listen in on the several smaller meetings within the larger one.

A question of semantics brought our attention together. The group assigned to parking and signs were tossing about phrases: Robert, they asked my son, what do you think? Do we put up a sign that reads "handicapped parking" ... or how about "disabled" ... or "other-abled" ... ? and they went through the inevitable euphemisms that have become part of contemporary language, disguising the visual known, words more comfortable to "others."

Robert reclaimed his wheelchair. "Use any terms you want to," he said, ". . . but the fact is you confuse people. No matter what terms you use, someone will not like it. Let's be clear. 'Handicapped' says it—nothing ambiguous about it."

Words! How struck I was by his ineluctable honesty, his fearless use of that fearful word, a word I never remember presenting to him and his sisters in my word-a-day-attached-to-the-refrigerator that began when they were infants—a word lurking nevertheless in his genes, in the healthy active boy, the young man he was until his mid-twenties when it surfaced, demanding our attention, our anguish, our recognition that our lives plunge forward, never to return to what was. In a letter received today he describes a library research class he took last year, a refresher course on words and research skills, a preparation for the law school classes he is taking now. "I loved that class, love being in the library!" he began, ". . . and if I complained as a child at all the reading you pressed on us . . . well . . . thanks!"

A new life—verbal, vocal, eloquent—beginning at age thirty-three.

He was listening in that "then" that seems eons ago, when he could still run, climb mountains, sail large sloops single-handed. He remembers. The ambiguity, the hesitancy, the overwhelming sense of the equivocal that permeates the reticence of so many people when they speak to, greet, are in the presence of a handicapped person, has escaped him. Beyond the dismay, the sheer terror, the awe of the progressive illness that has altered his life there are words to define it. Our use or abuse of words is what separates us—or clasps us close—to human life on earth.

It was summer, seven-and-a-half years ago. I had been thinking about the book I wanted to write. The hot humid heat of any Long Island summer leaned over the changing tides of Glen Cove Creek, shimmering just beyond my typewriter window, steaming the mudflats on the opposite shore and the wildlife preserve just behind it in the heron-filled trees. I counted thirteen great whites and eleven great blues; the shadows held countless tiny green herons, slightly larger night herons, and pecking at the shore were a half dozen snowy egrets, mating feathers silken whispers on their necks in the stifling heat.

During that hot summer of this book's gestation I struggled to conceptualize and define two thoughts—to translate an elusive abstraction—sound—into words; and to form a word-painting of something as ineffable as silence.

I tacked some thoughts from Thoreau's *Journal* to my window frame. In 1850 he wrote: "I walk over the hills to compare *great* things with small . . . ever and anon looking through a gap in the wood . . . to a more distant wood or hillside, painted with more coats of air." So many of the moments of these last seven-and-a-half years have been spent penetrating distant "coats of air," air shaken by ripples of sound, great and small, sound I cannot hear but want intimately to know beyond the scientific fact that it is *there*.

My husband is reading beside me, sitting on the floor of my office, leaning against my files. I touch his shoulder. He looks at me. I have turned off my hearing aids. Without them I cannot hear my own voice, the marbled sounds that I have come to know as "me." Even with them raised to their highest degree of efficiency, I do not know nuances of tone, resonance, all the color of articulation and rhythmical stress that distinguishes voice from voice. I concentrate on spoken utterances, lipreading, gathering intent and mood by watching expressions, the whole person.

Sabrina, a three-year-old Russian blue, born on a neighboring boat, is curled in my lap, purring, my fingers on his belly translating his murmurs of contentment to me. "What do I sound like?" I ask Harvey. "What is my voice like?" It is through language, the searching of it, that my silence becomes filled with imagery. The struggle to know sound again through words, to recall its finite reaches, its too-easily-forgotten elements, holds me to the vivid possibilities of language. Scientific knowledge, history, *all* knowledge is but words until we mingle *ourselves* with those unknown "coats of air," let that odd formation in our cerebellum, the *arborvitae*—the tree of life—engender our thinking processes, consider the cognizant known beyond visual observation. Scientific exposition, in defining and delineating the miraculous minutiae of our physical world, remains only words on paper unless that written scholarship, that perceived knowledge becomes more than the facts themselves, actually changes dimensions of thought.

Not everyone understands the compelling need for such a

quest. Annie Dillard said it best in her autobiographical *An American Childhood*: "... you do what you do out of your private passion for the thing itself." There are moments of realization, Dillard writes, that give "the dizzying over-real sensation of noticing that you are there. You feel life wipe your face like a big brush."

Harvey is thinking about my question—what does my voice sound like?

"Soft," he says, twirling his mustache, that musing look in his eyes. "Very soft ... with a little lilt to it ... bright, perky ... just a wonderful voice ... not a hush, low ... but not husky ... " He smiles, petting Anabel, our thirty-pound (male) feline, looking at me. "An absolutely beautiful voice ... "

His words—his love—falling on the air between us—a life-caress—that touch of the big brush ...

I did not want my book to evolve into a mere rendering of the eidetic lore of my research into sound and the perception of it; nor did I want this manuscript to be a memoir (that is another book).

I did want this search and the writing of it to be an unfolding, the ontogenetic adventure of a woman who has lost her hearing rather suddenly, discovering the world anew.

Thus ... there is no ending ... it is a continuing adventure ...

Winds whistle around mountain crags, across endless horizons of arid sands. Trees fall in forests. Icebergs crack open, break in two. Islands know the swish of leaves on tall trees, the rising slap of the tide, the jump and splash of fish. The song of a single whale singing to a mate is known to the intelligence of sea creatures for miles around it, in a place where the adjacent uninhabited land is a place we think of as silent.

Listening is hearing the imaginative.

We are all trees falling in the forest . . .